100 Stand-up Comics Talk about Learning Their Craft

in

The ULTIMATE GREEN ROOM

By

Barbara Corry

ISBN: 1-4392-0080-7
ISBN-13: 9781439200803

Visit www.booksurge.com to order additional copies.

For all comedians:

May you truly know
how much you can
brighten someone's day,
and
may you know how much
the laughter you bring
can mean in someone's life

Barbara

TABLE OF CONTENTS

ACKNOWLEDGEMENTS

To all the comics who were kind enough to sit down with me for interviews: Thank you. This book would not have come into being had you not been so willing to share your craft with me. In addition, your testimonials helped me to see my work through the comedian's eyes.

To the comics who provided the anecdotes that introduce and close each chapter: Thank you for adding so much color and humor to the book. Though brief, your anecdotes truly do flesh out the comedian's journey.

To Bob Fisher, owner of the legendary Ice House Comedy Club: Thank you for allowing me access to the comics, and thank you for your encouragement and generous support for this project.

To Kianoush Shirzad-Brand: You were there with me when the pilot study for this project started in 1987-88 at the University of Southern California, and you are still there for me today. Thank you for your artistic input, for your generous support of this project, and for your enduring friendship.

To Maryjane Liang: Thank you for taking the time to edit my work. And, thank you for thirty-two years of friendship, movies, laughter - and Jim and John.

To Linda Dorado: Thank you for lending your considerable art skills to my project. When you, Eric, and Jose came into my life in 1987, little did I know I would get to be a proud "Grand Aunt" to Aaron, Nikko, and Isaiah!

To Chris Mazzilli, Gotham Comedy Club: Thank you for taking time out of your busy schedule to sit down with me to discuss the New York comedy scene. Your observations were very helpful.

To Mitzi Shore: Thank you for granting me access to the comics at the Comedy Store for the pilot study in 1987–1988.

To my big brother, Guy, who always tried to make me laugh: On many occasions you nearly *tickled your little sister to death*, but you never failed to cheer me during the saddest of circumstances as we grew up.

To John Caparulo: Thank you for suggesting the title – and providing such a concise definition for my work.

PREFACE

I consider myself fortunate to have been born around the same time that television was in its infancy. I believe that my love and appreciation for comedy exists today, in part, because I got to "cut my teeth" watching the very best comedians that the new medium of television had to offer during the 1950s. Every week, Milton Berle, Jack Benny, Lucille Ball, Jackie Gleason, Red Skelton, and Burns & Allen were "appointment TV." As a child, I was regularly exposed to the comic genius of Sid Caesar, Imogene Coca, Carl Reiner, Steve Allen, and Ernie Kovacs. Every single Sunday, Ed Sullivan featured the finest comedians of the 1950s and 1960s. I firmly believe that I was imprinted by the brightest, most creative, and most talented comic minds of their generation as they explored what they could do with the new medium of television.

However, my love affair with comedy was also born of necessity, since I grew up in a home with alcoholism and domestic violence. When I say that the comedy of the early television comedians saved my life, it isn't an exaggeration. Comedy provided *relief* and it gave *hope* to one very sad little girl. Comedians made me laugh instead of wanting to cry all the time. Red Skelton, Jonathan Winters, and Sid Caesar all showed me that people could be warm and gentle and silly, and very funny, instead of cruel and violent.

The comedians of my youth literally taught me that there was something better out there (e.g., fun and lightheartedness in life), even if I was living in a hell called home.

My connection with comedy continued to flourish throughout the 1960s. The film comedies of Jerry Lewis became a staple of my Saturday afternoons from ages eight to thirteen. I can't count the number of times I saw *It's a Mad, Mad, Mad, Mad World* at the local theater back in 1964 (or how many times I've seen it since), and I would always come home from school and turn on *The Three Stooges*.

Allen King, Norm Crosby, Shelly Berman, Charlie Callas, Henny Youngman, Jackie Vernon, Danny Thomas, Totie Fields, Joey Bishop, Bob Hope, and Buddy Hackett entertained me throughout the 1960s. My teen years and twenties were filled with classic comedies such as *The Dick Van Dyke Show, Laugh-In, The Carol Burnett Show, The Mary Tyler Moore Show*, and *The Bob Newhart Show*. When I turned eighteen, I embarked on a Broadway show trip to New York. I was only in Manhattan for five days, but I saw four plays, I went to see The Dick Cavett Show, and I got to see Dom DeLouise in *The Last of the Red Hot Lovers*. When I turned twenty-one, I specifically went to see Phyllis Diller headline in Las Vegas.

In the late 1970s, I went to see the Sid Caesar retrospective, *Ten from Your Show of Shows* at the movie theater. I was amazed at how much of Caesar's work I remembered from my childhood. In later years, I got to see George Carlin and David Brenner in concert, and I closely followed the careers of Richard Pryor, Robin Williams, Jay Leno, and David Letterman. Johnny Carson entertained me for three decades with his monologues, comedy sketches, characters, and impersonations. I treasure my boxed set of *The Best of The Tonight Show*, along with my copies of the collected works of Lucille Ball, Kovacs, Skelton, and Caesar. I turn to them often because they never fail to make me laugh. To this day, I will not miss the current improvisational review at The Second City when I go home to visit old friends in Chicago.

During the 1980s, comedy played still another significant role in my life. In September 1983, my only brother died and I lost my mother to cancer eighteen months later. I desperately needed something to get me through my graduate courses at USC. The first thought that came to me sitting in class one day, was, "Do a project that involves stand-up comedy." Once again, in time of need, I turned to the men and women who had made me laugh and I did a project on comedians for that class. I subsequently interviewed 100 stand-up comics at the Comedy Store, the Improv, and the Ice House, and I performed a content analysis of the biographies of thirteen comedians. Thus were planted the seeds for this book.

In 1993, I started working at the Ice House Comedy Club in Pasadena, part-time on weekends, as a reservationist and cashier—for laughter and the love of comedy. I can honestly state that I am *never* happier than when I am sitting in the back of the show room after my shift watching a talented comedian perform. I have had the privilege of seeing virtually every act that has come through the Ice House (the oldest comedy club in the country) over the past fifteen years. Even when I've had a really bad day, sitting through a comic's set is such a natural mood elevator that I walk out of the showroom in a completely different frame of mind. Always.

I wrote this book because I wanted to learn more about the men and women who had made me laugh. I chose this project because I needed to be close to lots of laughter, and because I wanted to pass along the insights into the craft that the comics had so generously shared with me.

Moreover, as a sociologist I was curious about 1) the *comic* subculture, 2) how one chooses comedy as a profession, and 3) the process of professional socialization (e.g., how one acquires the rights, privileges, and responsibilities of a profession).

SOME FINAL THOUGHTS

There are three quotes in this book that particularly resonated with me. The first is comedienne Karen Babbitt's observation that for her, "*Stand-up comedy was survival. Stand-up is escapism—so that you have enough power to deal with other things in life.*" The second is Rodney Dangerfield's observation that, "*I started writing jokes not out of happiness but to go to a different place, because reality wasn't good to me.*" The third quote is comedian John Fox's description of *the loneliness and the sadness* experienced by many comics.

Over and over again in my life, I have turned to stand-up comedians for just these reasons; and this book is my way of saying a heartfelt "thank you" to all the men and women who have made me laugh. With apologies to all of the wonderful comediennes who have entertained me, I have chosen to use the pronoun "he" to refer to comics in the text for the sake of consistency and readability. No slight intended.

Rest assured that this project has been a labor of love, and that I have enjoyed every minute of being "a fly on the wall of the green room." The comics were a joy to interview. Their honesty and willingness to share their craft were *extraordinary*, and they have helped me to fully appreciate a passion of mine. They have made comedy a richer experience for me, and I believe that they have helped me heal a little bit more with every ounce of laughter they have provided. For all of these things, I am deeply grateful.

INTRODUCTION

I started this journey into the world of the stand-up comic by asking, "Who are stand up comedians—and how did they get that way?" Initially, I was curious about the early influences of those who become stand-up comics. Then, I became intrigued by the question: "What is the comic's equivalent of studying four years of accounting, engineering, or nursing—when there is no 'College of Cabaret Arts'?" I then set about documenting the *process* of how one moves from funny layperson to professional comedian. As I began to piece together each of the comic's career stages, I realized that I was also documenting the *road to headliner*—or how one achieves the highest rung in the comic's career ladder. And, in the process of talking about how they learned their craft, the comics revealed many insights into the performing art that is stand-up comedy. Comedy is not highly regarded as an art form, in part, because *comics don't appear to have a craft*. I decided then that I had to document the performing art I have loved all my life.

Comics were interviewed about *what* they learned, *when* they learned, and *how* they learned the craft at their various career stages. Special attention was given to the development of the comedian's comic persona, the evolution of his writing and performing skills, and those techniques devised by the comics to manage the difficult aspects of their work. The "life course" perspective, the sociological literature on professional socialization, and the concepts of "milestones" and "transition points" were all used to develop the interview questions and construct the *process* by which one becomes a professional comedian.

The comics I interviewed reflect the spectrum of those performing stand-up. They include "A" comics and "B" comics, veterans and newcomers, "fall-outs" and those who have been achieved success on *The Tonight Show*, *Star Search*, and *Last Comic Standing*. **You may recognize some of the comics I interviewed; *many you will not.*** What *is* important, and what the comics *all* share in common, is the *practitioner's intimate knowledge of the craft.* I selected each excerpt because of what it revealed about the art form or how one learns to be a stand-up comedian.

If the reader is looking for a collection of anecdotes by superstar comics, this is not that book: the vast majority of working comics are not "superstars." If you are curious about "how it all starts," if you enjoy "going backstage," or if you seek an understanding of the craft, then I think you will appreciate this detailed description of the comedian's "long, hard road to headliner."

<u>Overview</u>

Chapter One poses the question, "What must be there, in terms of natural ability, for someone to become a comedian?" Chapter Two explores several questions: 1) "How is the comic's natural talent first identified and/or nurtured within the family?" 2) "How is the comedian's talent shaped by his environment?" and 3) "What role does family play in shaping a comic's perspective and his choice of profession?" Chapters One and Two were drawn mainly from the biographies and autobiographies of comedians. *The reader may notice that they have a more academic "vibe."* I ultimately decided to include these "mini-chapters" for two reasons: 1) *they provide a life span perspective for the lives of comics* and, 2) *these chapters illustrate that, "not just anyone can do this job."*[71]

Chapters Three to Six strongly reflect "the voice of the comic" because they were taken directly from my interviews with 100 comedians. Chapter Three explores the comic's early performing efforts as he or she begins to participate in "open mic" nights during the Amateur Phase. Among the issues considered in the third chapter are overcoming stage fright, coping with failure ("bombing"), learning basic performing skills, and building one's first few minutes of material.

Chapter Four examines the comedian's formal entry into performing as he begins to work as an Opening Act. The major concerns at this stage include learning to write comedy, polishing a twenty-minute act, continuing to build minutes, learning to handle hecklers, and learning to perform for different audiences in different venues. This stage is roughly the equivalent of the freshman and sophomore ("general education") years in college. Opening Act is the career phase in which *the basics of the craft are learned.*

Chapter Five identifies those skills acquired as a middle act. This is the stage in which the comic more fully develops a comic persona, learns to edit his work, assembles a longer and more polished act, and hones the technical aspects of performing. In addition, as a feature act the comic learns to read and manage audiences, starts to work on the road, gets his first national television exposure, and begins to develop a following. This stage is roughly equivalent to the junior and senior years in college where the content of a major is emphasized. The middle act phase is *a cushioned spot that allows the performer to grow*. It is a stage where *the final touches are added to the performer*. In addition, *professional status is conferred and internalized* at this stage.

Finally, Chapter Six explores the process of moving from Feature Act to Headliner. Comics describe the growth that occurs as a Headliner in one's writing, performing, and audience skills. The sixth chapter further examines the increased responsibilities and many challenges that come with headlining. Comics share the best and the worst things about headlining, and they describe the business aspects of show business that they learn as a headliner. Headliners attain "master status" in their writing, performing, and audience management skills. By the time they headline, they have "paid their dues," and "earned their stripes." Headliners shoulder the responsibility of being the top bill and they reap the benefits of being featured on the marquee. This career stage is equivalent to the expertise one acquires during post-graduate education in one's field.

Because this book is about comedians, I felt it should be a *little* funny; therefore, I have introduced each chapter with humorous stories by comics that illustrate the funny side of a career in comedy. The featured topics include "the early years," "life on the road," "nightmare audiences," and "gigs from hell." I hope these anecdotes make you smile—and pique your curiosity about the material in the chapters they precede. Beyond their entertainment value, I believe they serve to "round out" the picture of a career in comedy. I hope you enjoy this journey into the world of the stand-up comic. I know I did!

CHAPTER 1

COMICS TALK ABOUT THE ROLE OF NATURAL TALENT IN BECOMING A STAND-UP COMIC

NATURALLY FUNNY

It's All in Your Perspective!

I was once asked, "What do you think makes a comic?" and I said, "It's the way you look at things." And that's true. I was driving down the highway, and we saw a three-legged dog. My wife said, "Oh, that poor thing!" I said, "Why? He's happy. He never has to lift his leg again. He's streamlined." She saw sad and I saw, "Hey, he can just lean over a little bit now and he's ready to go."

- Steve McGrew

Do I hear $1,100?

One night I was middling for Brad Garrett. There was a rowdy bachelorette party in the audience. I introduced Brad who came up on stage and shook hands as usual. Before I could leave the stage, however, Brad incited the girls to have me take my shirt off. I work out, so I did. Then, Brad turned to the bachelorette group and said, "And the bidding will begin at $1,000."

- Alonzo Bodden

Double Exposure

Sometimes when I perform, I do a joke about having a flat chest. One night while I was on stage, a woman in the audience stood up, pulled her blouse up, and bared her new, surgically enhanced breasts. She then proceeded to show her now ample bosom to the entire audience saying, "They only cost $3,000!" After a moment to let the audience settle down, I just looked at the woman and said, "Oh, I'm sorry. I'm not window shopping right now."

- Maryellen Hooper

A Comic's Prank

One night, I was headlining in the second show room at the Ice House. It was a wacky night, and I just thought it would be funny if I marched my entire audience through the main show room during a fellow comic's performance. I had this bandleader jacket and bandleader hat that I used to use as a prop whenever people came in late. I would put on the hat and jacket and make the late arrivals march behind me with a sign that said, "I was late; I'm sorry."

So, on a whim, I put on my bandleader jacket and hat, and I convinced the whole audience, about a hundred people, to get up and follow me. I led them up the aisle of the main showroom, across the stage, and out the side door—while Christopher Titus was performing on stage. Chris had no idea what was going on; he was speechless. After the show, Titus said, "I'm going get you back, someday." Then, the MC came up to me later and said, "Did anybody see the gay pride parade come through here?"

- Kevin Jordan

CHAPTER 1

COMICS TALK ABOUT THE ROLE OF NATURAL TALENT IN BECOMING A STAND-UP COMIC

You have to be born with a funny bone
for inspiration, and you must have a gift
for looking at the world through a funny, off center,
kind of prism. The rest is hard work, and refining
the product.
(TV interview, Mel Brooks)

Introduction to Chapter 1

The quotation by Mel Brooks above suggests that there are several components involved in the making of a stand-up comic. One component that Brooks and others cite as essential to becoming a professional comedian is natural ability. What *is* the role of natural talent among those who become stand-up comics?

Natural ability provides the comic with the instinct and the innate talent that the work requires. Family, peers, and environment form the comic's personality and shape one's "comic viewpoint" (see Chapter Two). Finally, the process of learning the craft involves *professional socialization,* i.e., acquiring the knowledge, skills, attitudes, and beliefs held closely within the profession. The "hard work" and "refining of the product" to which Mel Brooks refers are detailed in Chapters Three to Six as the comic moves from amateur to opening act to middle act to headliner.

Some Intriguing Notions Regarding the Role of Natural Ability in Becoming a Stand-Up Comic

Several comedians relate that stand-up comedy involves a specific ability to see and remember things of a comic nature. For example, comic Joey Gaynor recalls that he immediately memorized a hotdog bit performed by Alan King on the Ed Sullivan Show—and he remembers it to this day.

Other comics argue that you either have what it takes, or you don't. As one comic put it, "The comedic sense is inborn. It's not something you can describe or give somebody."[(21)]

Natural talent also includes the fact that comics are frequently bright, have good memories, and have a strong verbal orientation. For example, some comics display a special gift for word play, forming anagrams, or making puns. Other comedians are artists, and they hone the kind of imagination that is utilized in cartooning. Many comics are musicians, and musical talent often translates into sensitivity for the rhythm in language required by the work (i.e., these comics may have an innate sense of joke construction, and/or an "inner ear" for the timing required to deliver jokes effectively).

Often, the comic's skills are used to enhance his visible performance, such as when the comic does name associations when "working" the audience. Comic Jimmy Brogan, for example, recalls audience members' names and occupations and then he "weaves a thread" through the interactions that he has had with people in the audience. Some comics utilize their talent for reshuffling ideas, writing backwards, or for making unlikely connections into a trademark. Other comics, like Darren Carter, have a natural talent for mimicry. This talent for doing impressions allows Carter to "become" a hip-hop performer or a Latino character from the barrio, and do an uncanny imitation of a jack-in-the-box when an audience member randomly yells something out.

A professional comedian must be able to think quickly on his feet and mentally juggle many elements in ways the audience can't see. For instance, while he is performing, the comic is generally doing a number of other things such as deciding on the sequence of material, watching movement around the room, evaluating audience response to a new joke, and deciding which audience member to speak with next. In his autobiography, Dick Cavett describes the mental juggling that is required of a comedian/talk show host in addition to being funny:

> ... it looks as if all you have to do is follow the conversation. But you are also looking ahead, wondering whether to change the subject ... trying to decide if there is enough time in [the] segment to start something new, dying when the guest launches into a long story just before a commercial, and [you are] trying to remember what [the Guest] told you to ask him. [You are also] trying to decide which questions...to leave out, and [you are wondering] what signal did the stage manager just give you. (Cavett, 1974:255).

In addition, comics seem to have a talent for "milking" a humorous situation, and they seem to know how to make a great deal out of nothing. It has been said that comedians also have an instinct for *knowing exactly what to say, knowing how to magnify something*, and for *making something funny*. (See Croy's biography of Will Rogers, 1953:41).

Dick Cavett points out, however, that there is still a good deal of mystery to comic genius/comic instinct. He observes:

> Although you can know a lot about acting, there is still some mystery at the heart of great acting that has to do with being temporarily possessed. (p. 209) ... [This] is also at the heart of great comedy. ... [The performer] is not entirely in control of what has happened. It is akin to what the spiritualists call automatic writing. (p.210) ... That mystery, that visitation, is the thing performers fear losing because they don't know why they have it or what causes it. (Cavett, 1974:211)

Another element of natural talent is the "riveting presence" and "the special ability to communicate with audiences" that great comedians display. Nora Ephron has noted, "It is almost as though an essential part of the person is released when the red light goes on above the camera or when they hit the stage." (Ephron, 1968) Dick Cavett, for example, "would come together ... in front of an audience in ways that had not been glimpsed in rehearsal," and were even a surprise to him. (Cavett, 1974:148). Irving Fine (1976:271) describes a similar effect in the following anecdote about Jack Benny:

> Jack Benny would shed twenty years before your eyes as he'd straighten his shoulders, throw up his chin, and stride out on stage like a young trouper [when the orchestra would begin to play his theme, "Love in Bloom"].

> ... The stimulation of live audiences was like a shot of adrenaline for him.

And, as Bob Hope observed in Benny's eulogy, "Jack Benny didn't just stand on a stage, he owned it." (Fine,1976:18).

In sum, a significant part of what makes a stand-up comedian appears to be rooted in natural ability. Although one can learn to hold a microphone comfortably and one can acquire the experience necessary to manage an audience, a professional comedian must first have a natural instinct that provides the raw material for his work. He may also possess a specific talent (e.g., a talent for doing impressions or telling stories, etc.), and he will need the ability to master the writing and performing skills described in the chapters to come. However, as comedian Rudy Moreno observes:

> You have to have the funny bone. That is not learned. You can learn performing skills; but, I don't think you can learn to be funny.[(43)]

The specific form and content of one's humor takes shape over time, and stage time permits the honing of funny material; however, having the humorous instinct that tells a comic what to say or do *must be there first* in order to have a career in comedy.

> I think there are two types of natural ability. There's the writing natural ability. Then, there's the performing natural ability. I think most comics have one or the other—and they must work at the other. The great ones seem to have both.
>
> Tom Ryan

How and When Did You First Know You Were Funny?

I used to gravitate toward things that were funny. Also, people thought I was funny at school. Around the age of eleven or twelve, I would tell my friends stories. While I was telling the story, I would add my "take" on everything that was happening as the story progressed. Then, my friends would say, "Tell my mom and grandmother the story you just told me." Soon, I was making adults laugh. And, each time I told the story, I would think of something I could add. I'd think, "Oh, I can add a thing here that is funny." Basically, I was working out material at a really young age.

- John Caparulo

Always. Since I was a kid. My parents were very funny, and we all joked around the house. I was never funny in front of a group, though, because I was too shy. But, I could always make whomever I was with laugh. If I was really comfortable and it was a non-threatening situation, I could make my friends "pee their pants" in the back of the room. But, I would never get up in front of class. I didn't know how to be funny in front of a crowd until college. That was a breakthrough for me. When I could make my college friends laugh, I thought, "Wow, they really do find me funny!" I guess I always suspected and hoped.

- Don Friesen

I knew I was funny in high school. I wasn't a class clown, but I would always make a comment if something struck me as funny—and the class would laugh. My English teacher would laugh, too. There was another kid in class who thought he was funny, and sometimes he would make a comment also. One day in class, I made a comment. Everybody laughed. The teacher laughed, and he kept going. Then, this other kid made a comment but he didn't get a laugh. He did it again, and he tried it a third time. And, the teacher told him, "Stop interrupting class." Then the kid said, "How come you let Jim do it?" The teacher turned around and said, "Because he is funny." I felt bad for the kid, but I also thought, "Thank you very much!"

- James P. Connolly

I guess I knew I was funny when I could get out of a fight by making the other guy laugh. Then, when my mom asked me what I wanted to be, I told her, "I want to sit behind a desk." She said, "You mean like an accountant?" I said, "No, like Johnny Carson." I loved Johnny Carson because we were both from Nebraska.

- Jimmy Burns

I was always a big fan of stand-up. I would listen to Eddy Murphy and when the Rodney Dangerfield specials came on, I loved that. But, I never knew that I could actually be a stand-up comic. There weren't a lot of women doing stand-up at the time. When I was eighteen, my friends and I used to go dancing. When my other friends went for drinks, I would go into the comedy club because it was in the same building. I saw a couple women perform and thought, "I could do that." I had always been sarcastic; but I didn't know how to rein it in or write it.

- Tammy Pescatelli

CHAPTER 2

COMICS TALK ABOUT THE ROLE OF FAMILY AND ENVIRONMENT IN BECOMING A STAND-UP COMIC

Comic Insights on Family

"It's My Job To Make You Smile"

My mother says that I started doing comedy to make her smile. I was in the kitchen one day, and I said, "Mom, how come you always look like this?"—and I drew a sad face—"and how come you never look like this?"—and I drew a happy face. She says from that point on, it was my job to make her smile. On the other hand, my father could always make my friends laugh. He could always make my girlfriends laugh. I was a little jealous of that. I wanted to do that. Plus, anybody who grows up in a big family knows that you're fighting for attention. But, I would bet that every comic gets material from his family, or has a wacky mother, a crazy father, or a goofy uncle whom they feel is the reason that he is a comic.(54)

- Kevin Jordan

"Gifts from My Parents"

My father was Irish and he had a great, off-kilter sense of humor. He was always saying things that, even as a kid, I found funny. My dad also enjoyed playing practical jokes. My mom, who was Italian, also had a wonderful sense of humor. She just encouraged me to act, sing, and be involved in the arts.

My dad also influenced the *type* of humor I do. He taught me to respect people's nationalities. He told me, "If you are going to tell a joke, it's okay to poke fun at the system, or politicians, or things that hurt people; but don't insult other groups." Then, when my dad was sick, I turned to comedy as a coping mechanism.

Music and a sense of humor were also my way of getting by in my neighborhood. I had to defuse a lot of taunting as a kid. A lot of the insults the kids would hurl are things that I use in my act today. In the back of my mind I knew I wanted to be a performer. I would be hurt by their insults, but I would say to myself, "Okay, I will use that some day."(52)

- Joey Gaynor

"To Do What Makes You Happy"

When I started doing comedy, my father said, "Go ahead and do it." My mother said, "What's wrong with you?" But, all in all, they were very supportive. When you see somebody doing a job that they love and have always been destined to do, you support that. How many of us truly love our jobs? I worked for the gas company for seventeen years and hated every day of it. To have an opportunity to do comedy—something I did in the classroom, on the playground, and when I was hanging with the guys—has been great!(43)

- Rudy Moreno

"My Friends and Teachers Told Me So"

I knew I had a funny streak. My childhood friends always said I had timing. My speeches in college were funny. My professors told me I should be a comedian. I worked for the government for a while, and I felt like I just couldn't spend my life doing that job. So, I decided to try comedy.(62)

- Larry Omaha

A GAP AS BIG AS THE GRAND CANYON

Comics have a huge, huge gap in their egos. There is a huge piece missing from when they were children. It's a piece of self-worth that was filled in for others on a continuous basis with things like, "Good, honey," "That was nice, honey," or "Oh, I like that, honey."

Rodney Dangerfield said it best, "Tell me that I'm wonderful. Tell me I'm okay. Tell me I'm as good as the rest." These are the teeny niceties that most children get—and we comics didn't.

I find that the common thread among comics is that we come from super-critical families or neglectful families or, sometimes, abusive families. It's the reason that, as adults, we have this huge, gaping hole inside. It's the reason we become such ego-maniacs, and the reason that it takes 300 people applauding to fill that hole in our soul.

We have a gap the size of the Grand Canyon and now, as adults, "That's nice, honey" doesn't fill it. We need 300 people applauding wildly to bring us up to par with somebody who has grown up with all those little niceties.[20]

Karen Babbitt

CHAPTER 2

COMICS TALK ABOUT THE ROLE OF FAMILY AND ENVIRONMENT IN BECOMING A STAND-UP COMIC

The comedians I spoke with indicate that both positive and negative experiences with family had a significant influence on their choice of profession.

Positive Contributions by Families

Family is the setting where the child's natural talent is first displayed—and is first recognized. Through the reactions of parents, siblings, and friends, the child first learns *he is funny* and *he can have an impact on others*.

The parents of some comics report that there was an early and acute fascination with anything that was funny. As early as age four, some comics displayed a precocious talent for imitating comedians they had seen.[52]

Some comics recalled *knowing* that they had a talent for comedy when they would perform skits for their parents and friends (e.g., Milton Berle, 1974). Even at a tender age, these comics *knew* that they had been funny and *felt gratified* that they apparently had a talent for making others laugh.

Many comics reported that, from childhood on, being funny was a way of securing parental attention—a "look at me, Mommy" phenomenon. For some comics, being the class clown was a way to connect with peers. For other comics, family was the first place they discovered that being funny could bring them the attention they enjoyed or craved. As John Wing notes: "I come from a big family, and we're all rather attention-getting people."

Family also is the first place where the comic's sense of humor was nurtured, both directly and indirectly. Some parents actively encouraged their child's early display of talent and steered them along professional lines (e.g., Milton Berle, 1974). Other families did not "push" the child toward show business. Instead, they unknowingly provided an environment filled with humor for the young child.

For example, some comics report growing up surrounded by wildly funny family members. Other comics report growing up surrounded by laughter and funny stories. Still others recall growing up within families who listened to comedy albums, watched lots of comedy on television, and attended comedy films and concerts as a family. As comic John Caponera recalls, "I grew up in a family where all my of my uncles and my grandfather told jokes all my life. So, I always knew how to tell a joke."

Family can be a source of love and encouragement that serves the comic well later in life, e.g., family members can instill diligence, ambition, and support the comic's dreams. Family also can provide the confidence that allows the comic to pursue a career that is not "9-to-5," and family can engender traits such as discipline and responsibility. These behaviors often can make a critical difference between success and failure later in one's career.

Family is the place where the comic first learns to use comedy as a coping mechanism. Some comics learned that humor was a way of coping with pain (e.g., "You are brought up to make fun of life, because otherwise you cry."). Other comics learned that comedy was an excellent way to defuse conflict (e.g., "Having a ready laugh gets you out of a lot of tough spots, and it can make instant friends out of enemies."). Still other comics learned that humor was a way of coping with being "different" physically, such as being fat, skinny, tall, having a flat chest, or being disabled, (e.g., "It's easier to have people laugh *with* you instead of *at* you.").

Some comics learned that humor was a way of coping with the crazy, illogical things we experience each day. Comics who specialize in observational comedy frequently draw on this perspective. The comedy of funny men like the Marx Brothers and the Three Stooges is a humor that stems from a heightened sense of the ridiculous and the absurd. They have a talent for doing things "over the top." These comics learned that bringing some silliness into the world is an important thing. Their experiences fostered a belief that people take themselves too seriously and that life is frequently much too sad. They came to feel that our daily lives are filled with so much pressure that things *need* periodic depressurizing. Through their families, these comics came to define humor as serving *an important function for getting through life*.

Some anecdotes also suggest that specific elements of one's comic style are also learned within the family. This is particularly evident in the cases of Richard Pryor, Paul Rodriguez, and David Brenner as illustrated below.

Richard Pryor's father, for example, was "devastatingly funny—and he would tell the truth even if people didn't want to hear it." Pryor also learned that, "even though it might shock, the words are true, and that this can become a 'language within a language' that is so to-the-point that it makes pictures in your mind" (Pryor, 1987). These very words also described much of Richard Pryor's work.

Paul Rodriguez learned the power of language from his father. He learned that a parent's anger—and the guilt it instilled—could be sharper than any knife (Borns, 1987:113).

Rodriguez also learned that while physical pain goes away, "words stay in your mind." (Borns 1987:114) Rodriguez has described comedy as "his weapon." These early experiences taught him the value that language holds for influencing people, and he has used the stage as a means to fight poverty and discrimination.

David Brenner states that his father is "extremely funny." (Borns, 1987:112) He adds that he "got his father's genes" and that he [even] inherited his "[comic] style from his father." (Borns, 1987:113) Comic Nick Gaza also recalls having a very funny family, and states that he looked at performing comedy as "something that seemed like it would be fun." Joey Gaynor states that both of his parents had "slightly off-center senses of humor." When asked by Oprah Winfrey if everyone in their family was funny, one of the younger Wayans brothers responded, "Yes. My mother is Richard Pryor with breasts."

The talent for being a "born storyteller" also appears to have its roots in the family. Some performers can stand on stage and talk comfortably for hours. Many of these performers credit family members who were both extremely funny and fascinating. These comics seem to have "inherited" the ability to make the most out of any anecdote. When they recount a story, they are able to make it seem more vivid, more intense, and more fascinating, and they are able to make the story grow funnier as it goes along (e.g., Jack Parr, Bill Cosby, and Gabe Kaplan).

Several comics noted that the comedian's ambition often can be rooted in one's environment. Several comics attribute their drive for success to their determination to overcome the poverty they knew while growing up.

Finally, other comedians are influenced by the "the American Dream" and the lure of making money, owning a beautiful home, and becoming a star.

Negative Influences of the Family or Environment for Comics

Comedians have been described as a group of individuals who are, by definition, insecure. George Carlin, for example, once observed that "Comedians are [individuals who] are looking for a lot of things that begin with A's: attention, approval, audiences, applause, approbation, affirmation, and acceptance." (Borns, 1987:258)

Other comics, however, disagree with the idea that all comics were abused or neglected children. Because of the many positive family experiences cited above, and because the family experiences of some comics do not include an abusive childhood, it is probably inaccurate to say that the comedian develops *only* as a result of great unhappiness. Nevertheless, the painful childhood experiences reported by many comics suggest that they do have a significant impact on their subsequent personal and professional lives.

Although reasons for personal insecurity may vary, many comics have experienced weakened bonds with family. Some comics reported growing up in severely dysfunctional families. In other cases, they grew up with alcoholism in the family, or experienced physical abuse. For example, in Smith's 1986 biography of Bill Cosby, he reports that some of Cosby's early childhood experiences were extremely painful. Haskins (1984) reports that Richard Pryor grew up in his grandmother's brothel.

Comedian Rodney Dangerfield drew on a lifetime of pain, even as he made audiences laugh. Despite his very solid success later in his life, Dangerfield once told a reporter in 1997, "I have never been happy. My whole life has been a downer." Dangerfield recalled:

> When I was young, I had to deliver groceries to the homes of the kids I went to school with. I had to go to the back doors to make the deliveries. It was embarrassing. I felt like they were better than I was. My self-esteem was very low. Things like that stay with you, where you never think you are as good as anybody else. (McLellan, *Los Angeles Times*, Obituary, 10-6-04)

McClellan reports that Dangerfield also recalled:

> At age fifteen, I began writing jokes; not out of happiness, but to go to a different place because reality wasn't good to me. Show business was like a "fix," and I had to have it to escape reality. (McLellan, *Los Angeles Times*, Obituary, 10-6-04)

Rodney Dangerfield later built a career on the phrase, "I don't get no respect." He created a very successful act by joking about his troubles and insecurities; he became an "everyman" by putting his finger on the ways we all can feel "put down" or "put upon" by others from time to time.

Comedian Milton Berle also expressed an unhappiness in his life. At the end of his autobiography, Berle states, "Next time around, I want to laugh." (Berle, 1974)

For many of the men and women who make us laugh, comedy is a way to cope with the pain they experienced. The intimacy that was lacking in his family may drive the comic to obtain emotional sustenance from the audience and/or from self-medication.

The oldest jokes in human history involve rebellion and subjects that are taboo. Comedians who do political comedy have a propensity for questioning things and challenging the status quo. Some comics openly defy authority or express aggression in ways most of us do not. Does the pent-up anger and hostility that drives the humor of such comedians stem from a dysfunctional family, poverty, the painful awkwardness of adolescence, or feeling like they don't fit?

Even where abuse was not part of their experience, some comics report having had a strained relationship with their parents especially, but not exclusively, with their fathers. For example, several comics (identities withheld) recall:

- My father never told me that he was proud of me.
- My mom never said, 'I love you.'
- Nothing I ever thought, did, or said was right (or good enough).

Several comics state that they never felt like they had much in common with their parents. In such cases, some comics turn to friends for understanding and companionship. Friends understood the love they had for show business when their parents did not. Friends also understood their dreams, their love for exploring new things, and their desire to have exciting adventures.

Many comics found a way to fill a weakened bond with family through performing. In such cases, the "love of many" may become a substitute for the intimacy that the comic lacked within his family of origin—or in subsequent adult relationships. As one comic put it, "When they laugh, they 'get' me." Hence, the laughter of audiences signifies understanding and acceptance—on a very large scale.

Family and/or environment can also be the source of cynicism in a comic's perspective on life. For example, Dick Cavett states that he developed a cynical attitude about politics in high school when he "saw how easy it was for a totally uncommitted personality to give off [an air] that gets votes." (Cavett, 1974:32). This kind of cynicism may turn up later in a wry or sarcastic comic attitude.

A painful childhood also can serve to broaden a comic's perspective. Extreme experiences can give the comic insight into social problems and may permit him to see flaws in the social fabric. The choice by many comedians to include social and political commentary, along with the tendency of comics to provoke or ridicule sacred cows, seems to be rooted here.

A conflict-ridden family may even prepare a comedian to survive the battle conditions of his calling, i.e., learning to persevere under adverse conditions at home may help the comic survive the experience of "bombing" in his early career. Conflict in the family may also show up in the comic's propensity to prove himself—over and over again in front of audiences.

Finally, Karen Babbitt reports that her family taught her humor as a survival mechanism:

> My mom was in the prison camps. She was at Auschwitz. There are four comics I know who are second generation survivors. Those odds are phenomenal. The common thread is that the way people stayed sane in the camps was with humor. That's what was handed down to us children. For me, stand-up comedy was survival. Stand-up is escapism—so that you have enough power to deal with other things in life.[20]

In sum, while natural ability must be present in order to perform professionally, family and environment play an important role in the development of the prospective stand-up comic's attitude, motivation, and his choice of vocation.

"Funny Can't Be Learned; But The Craft Must Be"

Funny is not something you can learn. It's something that is already there that needs honing. Maybe it's something that's instilled in you from your upbringing; but I would say that 75 percent of comedy is something that you can't learn, and there is about 25 percent that is *timing, delivery, and writing.*[3]

- Jim Shubert

> In the beginning, it's sheer tenacity, and you're learning how to overcome the fear...You're nervous and scared. You want everybody to like you, and you really don't know how to do that. Then, you go through a long process where you're finding your your stage presence, your character, and your attitude.
>
> Eddie Merrill

CHAPTER 3

THE AMATEUR PHASE: 0 – 1 YEAR
STARTING OUT

IT CAN BE SUCH "FUN" WHEN YOU ARE STARTING OUT

A Glimpse into the Future?

One night when I was starting out, I went to a club in Southern California. There was one guy in the audience who kept heckling the comedian and giving him a really hard time. And the comedian said, "You think this is so easy; come on up here." So, the guy got up there. He literally grabbed the microphone away from the comic, and he started to insult people in the audience. The MC had to go up on stage, forcibly grab the microphone away from the guy, and settle things down. And, I'm sitting in the audience thinking, "What the hell am I getting myself into?"

- Kareem Matthews

Throw Money, Not Food. Please!

I was doing a comedy show in the back of a Chinese restaurant back East. There was a girl on stage and she was not doing well. The whole crowd was drunk and rowdy. The crowd was already belligerent when she went up, but in the middle of a joke someone from the crowd hurled a spare rib that whizzed past her head and hit the curtain on the back of the stage. The spare rib had so much sauce on it that it slowly slid down the curtain. By the time the spare rib had slid down to about her waist, the comedienne said, "Okay, I've had enough," and she just walked off the stage.

- Dan Smith

One Single, Solitary Laugh

One night I just had a terrible set. No matter what I did, the audience just wasn't laughing. I was dying up there. That night, I only got one laugh: I was staring at the audience and I was staring at the lights, and finally I said to them, "You should see this from my end." The whole room just erupted.

- Juan Canopii

Now That's High Anxiety!

On one amateur night at the Ice House, this woman was performing and all of a sudden she collapsed. She crawled to the back of the stage and curled up into a fetal position and she just stayed there. Nobody knew what to do. The producer, Dave McNary, finally went up on the stage and the other comics went on with the show—with this woman curled up on the floor in the corner. She had apparently had this anxiety attack, and she was just frozen; she couldn't move. We had to have someone come get her after the show.

- Kevin Jordan

Yo, Cut Me Some Slack—I'm Up Here Trying to Learn!

One time I performed at an open mic at a bar in downtown Manhattan. This venue mostly catered to musicians, but comedians were known to slip into the mix. It's definitely not easy to "kill" in front of a crowd of other entertainers who are more concerned with their own performance. Then again, I say you haven't really lived until the lady behind the bar yells, "Put the music back on!" while you're stumbling through your set.

- Christine Sparta
Staff writer and Columnist
Home News Tribune
East Brunswick, NJ

CHAPTER 3

THE AMATEUR PHASE: 0 – 1 YEAR
STARTING OUT

The open mic phase is about going up on stage, being willing to fail, learning to live with failure, learning how to deal with the rejection, getting comfortable on stage, and starting to learn what the craft is all about.
Bill Kalmenson

Introduction to the Amateur Phase

After deciding to try stand-up comedy, the aspiring comic typically begins by performing at open microphone nights. Here the comic begins the process of "testing the water" to find out whether he is suited for a career in comedy.

Until the 1980s, a student might take acting classes or hone his skills in improvisation, but there were very few classes or workshops in which one could specifically learn to perform stand-up comedy. Comics report that until very recently, the novice learned stand-up by "performing wherever he could convince an owner to let him perform." Stand-up comedy folklore is replete with stories about the run down bars (also known as "toilets" or "one-nighters"), in which the craft has been learned.

Since the 1970s, increasing numbers of comics have learned their craft in comedy clubs. Clubs such as The Improv and The Comedy Store are known as "showcase" clubs, and they function as comedy "colleges" where novices can learn the craft and veteran comics can showcase for agents and rehearse new material. The pay in showcase clubs is relatively low; however, positions in such clubs are sought because of the networking opportunities and stage time they afford the comic.

Today, there are a growing number of classes that specifically offer instruction in stand-up comedy. Students may learn a variety of stand-up skills in these workshops. They may learn the basics of comedy writing or gain some confidence on stage. They can also learn ways to hold a microphone, practice a classic comedy routine, and rehearse their new material. Comedian Daniel Nainan provides one example of comics who have benefited from stand-up classes:

> The instruction I received in class helped me to avoid a lot of mistakes. I found that classes were the best place to try new material because there are people from all walks of life there, just like your average audience. ...Their reaction is often a better indicator than performing only for other amateurs. Some "open mic" comics are bitter or jaded and purposely try not to laugh. This can be very damaging for the beginning comic.
>
> With comedy classes, it's a more supportive environment. Also, with classes you get to perform at a real comedy club as your "final exam." Often, you'll have the support of friends and relatives in the audience.[67]

Despite the growth in the number of stand-up classes, many comics argue that stand-up is an art form that is self-taught. One comic describes his early training as "learning by trial and error"[13] and another as "learning via the school of hard knocks."[1] Comedienne Kathy Buckley describes the importance of performing for live audiences this way:

> There is no better place to learn your craft than in front of an audience. They are your best judges. That's how you find out what is going to work. Your audience will help you to be the best comic you can be.[62]

For the most part, the aspiring comic today still learns his craft by going up on stage and performing in front of club audiences on "open mic" nights. Performing before an audience is the only way amateur comics can determine if they like doing stand-up and whether they are effective at it. The live feedback from audiences is also critical to developing a comic persona and refining one's material.

Open Microphone Nights

Currently, most performing experience is acquired by performing at "open mic" nights. One of the first things the aspiring comic must do is to learn where to go and how to get access to stage time. Comics find out about the "pot luck nights" around town from a variety of sources, including daily newspapers and weekly entertainment papers. Newcomers also learn of amateur nights through trade paper announcements, word of mouth, or having visited a comedy club as a patron.

"Open microphone nights" or "pot luck nights" are evenings (or portions thereof) that are set-aside for amateurs each week at the clubs. On "open mic" nights, anyone can sign up to perform on stage for a period ranging from three to five minutes. "Open mic" protocols vary by club. First timers are given preference at many clubs. At some clubs an aspiring comic may "show up and sign up" at an appointed time. At other clubs, lottery style numbers are used to assign performing slots to amateurs. Several comics recall lining up early in the day to get a lottery number for just a chance at one of eleven "open mic" spots that night at a major club in New York.[1, 2]

Some aspiring comedians secure jobs at a comedy club. They perform such functions as door security, food server, or cocktail waitress. Such jobs provide income and allow the aspiring comic to have "hang out" privileges at the club. These jobs also permit the amateur to observe the other comics and to "see what comedy is all about." Finally, working at the club provides visibility for the newcomer, a chance to interact with other comics, and an occasional opportunity to get up on stage that other amateurs don't have.

During their "open mic" phase, comics report supplementing these appearances with stage time at various talent nights or "comedy nights" at local bars and restaurants. Other early performing efforts also included performing along the beach, in small coffee houses, in large parks, or in central city squares. Getting "stage time"—in whatever form they could get it—became one of the central concerns of the comic's amateur stage.

The "open mic" phase is a tough apprenticeship for the aspiring comic, both physically and emotionally. It is an experience that the comics liken to a "trial by fire" ordeal that brutally tests one's courage and persistence. As comic Don Friesen describes it, "You are the least polished at your craft. You have the least material, and you have the least going for you. Basically, you have the worst possible situation in which to succeed." Or, as another comic put it, "You have to be willing to be bad to become good; and if you are not willing to do that, you don't have what it takes."

The "open mic" phase is demanding *physically* because most aspirants still have day jobs. As newcomers in the club setting, amateurs may have to wait until the wee hours of the morning to go on stage—with an audience composed of a handful of (drunk) customers and a few comics in the back of the room. Performing on a regular basis while holding down a job can take its toll on the aspiring comic's health.[4] In addition, for some would-be comics, ten minutes on stage can be draining. Performing stand-up comedy may require more physical stamina than the amateur expects and, even after a short set, the "open mic" comic may feel like he has just put in eight hours at hard labor.[59]

The amateur phase also is difficult *emotionally* for the aspiring comic. First, performing can be hard because of the performance anxiety many amateurs experience. Second, this phase is difficult because of the emotional impact that "bombing" has on the newcomer. Third, the amateur stage is challenging because the aspiring comic is immediately placed in front of audiences without finely tuned material, without a well-defined comic persona, and without well-developed performing skills. The amateur is forced to sink-or-swim in front of critical audiences who may be drunk and rowdy. One comic likens the process to getting up on stage and learning how to play a guitar (from scratch) in front of paying customers. Fourth, the "open mic" phase also requires the aspiring comic to face a great deal of waiting. As the "new kid on the block," an amateur may wait around until after midnight to go on for three minutes, and then get bumped from the line-up if a veteran, star, or friend of the owner comes in and wants stage time.

The "open mic" phase can last anywhere from a few months up to one year, depending on the amount of stage time the amateur gets and the previous experience he or she brings to stand-up. For example, getting a lot of stage time in the supportive environment of a small club, having been an actor, having taken classes in improvisational comedy, or having performed from an early age, can provide the comic with stage presence and experience with audiences. These elements tend to speed up the length of time the amateur spends at this stage (e.g., eight months versus fifteen months).

Progress at this stage also can depend on the aspiring comic's maturity, motivation, and his or her psychological readiness to do stand-up. According to several comics, laziness, a marked lack of maturity, and extreme insecurity can mean that the comic will spend relatively more time at this stage than others (e.g., two years instead of one year).

Several comics describe having what they termed as "false starts" at performing stand-up. They made attempts at performing and then stopped.[5, 6] To paraphrase two of the comics, they felt they "were not psychologically ready." Other comics defined this readiness as "having the willingness to fail," and "being ready to commit to the craft."

On the other hand, for amateurs who have some life experience or come to performing with the nucleus of a character, doing stand-up can be "very freeing" and it can allow them to express themselves in a way they had not previously experienced.[43, 42, 23] For example, Frank Carrasquillo recalls, "I entered comedy as a repressed talent. When I finally went up, it all just came out pure and beautiful, and I had a natural presence almost immediately." Rocky LaPorte agrees that when it goes well, the first time can be an extraordinary experience for the amateur comic:

> The first time I went up, the laughs were like a drug. I knew right away. I said, "Man, this is what I want." It was

> an amazing, overwhelming thing. I said, "Holy Cow! To know that I have this effect on people." And then there were the waves of laughter coming at you. I thought, "This is an awesome thing."[42]

What Happens During the Amateur Phase

The major skills and experiences of the Amateur Phase are:

- Overcoming the fear of performing
- Surviving the experience of "bombing"
- Coping with the aftermath of "bombing"
- Learning techniques to avoid failure
- Learning basic performing skills
- Learning stage etiquette
- Putting your first ten minutes of material together
- Developing stage comfort
- Learning to interact with audiences
- Showcasing
- Moving from "open mic" to opening act
- Getting the first paying jobs

Overcoming the Fear of Performing (a.k.a., "Learning How Not to Vomit")

Masking the intrinsic fear of performing is one of the most difficult tasks confronting most novice comics. Comics readily acknowledge the fear they felt when they first began doing stand-up. The physical manifestations of this fear included nausea, dry mouth, shaky knees, sweaty palms, and diarrhea. The following quote from one comedienne illustrates how intense this fear can be:

> The first six months, I was nauseous every morning. I had butterflies in my stomach if I knew I had to get up on stage that night. I couldn't eat right all day. I stood there with a memorized three minutes or six minutes of material and just tried to say it and hoped somebody would laugh. I was not "relating to" or "being with" anybody—I was, like, in another space. I'm sure I was very stiff. I was, like, mouthing words. I knew words were coming out of me because I had memorized them, but I was petrified.[8]

Male comics also experience stage fright. One male comic describes his decision to perform solo on stage as "overcoming the plunge of terror."[2] Another comic describes his anxiety this way:

> The five minutes before you go on, that's the toughest. Will you die? Will you have a horrible feeling? Will they not like you? Will you become a

> mouthful of marbles? Millions of things like that go through your mind.[31]

Feelings of utter isolation on stage and personal rejection constitute a palpable threat to one's self-esteem. Therefore, one of the amateur comic's major tasks is to overcome performance anxiety. Getting past the fear is important for several reasons:

- Fear interferes with concentrating on your material.
- Fear clouds your judgment of audience response.
- Audiences will sense fear, become uneasy, and may begin to heckle.

Several comics estimate that it can take between 75 and 300 performances before the young comic begins to feel comfortable on stage.

Some comics characterize "getting by the fear" as a challenge or as an exercise in order to conquer their fear. As one comic put it:

> You learn that you just have to become intimate with terror. You have to make bold and look at terror like a dog that you are going to pet and say, "Yes, I'm shaking. I'm nauseous. I'm terrified. But I am going to take a breath in the middle of all this and try to take a step up from the terror."[2]

Several comics indicate that overcoming fear is a matter of becoming desensitized by repeated trips to the stage.

Other comics indicate that it becomes a matter of finding the techniques to overcome fear that work for you. Both male and female comics indicate that they utilized a variety of means to get over their fear, including: meditation, meticulously planning out every minute of that day, carefully planning their set, and concentrating hard on their opening line. Diane Nichols describes some of the techniques that she has observed comics employ to get past their fear:

> I've seen guys sit in a chair and take deep breaths. Other guys look at their notepads intently. Some start walking around listening to a recording of their act before going on stage. All to get in the right "head space." Bobby Slayton used to blast the Rolling Stones in the condo as he dressed. It's the comic's version of "Gentlemen, start your engines."[(4)]

Many comics pace in the hallways or do warm up exercises before going on stage to dissipate their nervous energy. Some comics go off by themselves to collect their thoughts, get into "character," "turn on the energy," or summon the courage to go on stage. Comedian Rudy Moreno recalls trying to self-medicate his early fear with alcohol:

> The biggest mistake I made was to try to calm my nerves by drinking. One night, I went on stage and completely forgot what I had practiced all day long. Ever since then, I've stayed away from alcohol.[(43)]

Although conquering fear is a common task for most novices, not all comics experienced fear with the same intensity. For instance, one comic states:

> I get a case of the butterflies every now and then. It was never a big problem for me because I had been doing magic since I was ten. I was just always performing for people.[3]

However, the fact remains "No comic is equally impressive to all audiences at all times." There are no guarantees of success every time they go on stage—even for the pros. For instance, when Jerry Seinfeld ended his television series, he retired all of his old stand-up material and he began to build an hour of new material from scratch. As documented in his film, *Comedian*, Seinfeld, too, confronted performance anxiety night after night in comedy clubs all around New York, until he had perfected a new, hour-long act that could be performed confidently on television and in large concert venues nationally.

Because failure is always a possibility, performance anxiety is something that both novices and seasoned performers must come to accept as part of the job. As one comic describes it, "There will always be 'off nights' and crowds who aren't 'your' crowds. In addition, there will always be situations where the stakes are higher and the fear is stronger [e.g., having a set on *The Tonight Show* with Jay Leno or *The Late Show* with David Letterman]."

Some novices even come to regard their fear as useful. Several comics report that they functioned better when their backs were up against the wall. Others state that they had written some of their best stuff when they were under the most difficult circumstances, or they tried to use the fear to sharpen their performance.

Whether he experiences a lot of fear or a little, conquering performance anxiety is essential for the young comic to succeed. It is only after he has gotten past his terror that he can grow as a performer. He will then begin to notice more things about the room, develop greater ease in interacting with audiences, begin to *listen* to the audience, bring out more of his personality, and develop the confidence to allow his own unique brand of humor to emerge. Moreover, the fear management skills that the comic develops as an amateur will serve him his entire career. Therefore, those amateurs who move on to performing professionally must find a way to overcome their fear.

Confronting Other Fears

In addition to stage fright, comics spoke of other fears that they had during their early performing efforts. Comedian Tom Ryan, for example, was "concerned that comedy was an insider's club and that he wouldn't be able to crack it." In addition, Ryan was initially concerned that "comics would be a cold group with whom I would not get along." Neither fear proved true. Finally, like many amateurs, Ryan was also unsure whether he could handle hecklers, and he questioned how well he would handle "bombing."

Encountering and Surviving the Experience of Bombing

The comics liken their early performing experiences to "the tales of the early Christians being thrown to the lions." The amateur is sent up on stage without polished performing skills, without carefully crafted material, and without a well-developed comic persona or comic attitude. The result is predictable: initially, frequently, the amateur "bombs." His timing is off. He does not yet present the material with consistency or confidence. He has yet to learn how much difference changing one word or pausing one beat can mean in getting a laugh. The aspiring comic has yet to learn the craft.

As one comic describes it, "the only way you learn to do it right, is by doing it wrong a thousand times and by dying a thousand deaths." Still another comic recalls, "*You learn by feeling all of the emotions that happen when you are not getting things right on the button*."

Comic Diane Nichols describes a typical performing pattern for a newcomer this way:

> At first, you have a thing where you do an okay show, then you bomb the next two, and then you do okay on the third, and then you bomb for three. Then, you do a real good one out of nowhere. After a while of bomb-good-bomb-bomb-good, you get to a point where you've learned how to put on a funny show.[4]

Comic Tim Jones describes the learning curve for an aspiring comic this way:

> You bomb. Then you don't bomb quite as much. Then, you go home with that five-minute tape, and you get three laughs in five minutes—and you consider that a great set.[12]

Until he improves, however, the amateur comic must endure many bad nights of "dying" on stage. The late Steve Allen once defined dying as:

> A state of sweat-drenched ineptitude characterized by total and humiliating silence so overwhelming that even hecklers are usually ashamed to speak. (Allen, 1981)

Veteran comic Jeff Altman recalls an early experience with "bombing" this way:

> One night when I was first starting out and I was a Grade "C" comedian, I followed Richard Pryor. The best comedian in the world gets on stage and I had to follow him. I did not get one whimper. I just got up there, said all these words, and got off. It was terrible. Very embarrassing. You see, laughter is an instant recognition of, "I'm good." No laughter is an instant recognition of "I'm a failure." You're told immediately. It's a no-nonsense business.[14]

Another comic adds the following perspective on bombing:

> When you don't get laughs, you look stupid. It's not like doing a C- soliloquy from Shakespeare. If you do less than a great thing in Shakespeare, the audience can just sit there and clap politely at the end, and you will get fifteen different opinions in the lobby.

> For the comic, if there are no laughs it's obvious to everybody—and there is nothing more painful to observe or experience.[2]

Over and over, comics will tell you that there is *nothing more painful to experience than "bombing."* When he "dies" on stage, the amateur is up there alone, with the cold fear, the dead silence, and hecklers just waiting to pounce. Comedian Fritz Coleman provides the following example of the feelings that can follow bad sets early on:

> When you are starting out and they don't laugh, you just stumble off and you feel like you have been punched in the diaphragm. Stage fright is the biggest thing to get over, and just getting that confidence on stage is a major victory.
>
> Lenny Bruce's Mom said, "The real skill in this business is learning to die with dignity." Learning to handle bombing with aplomb—either by talking yourself out of it, or by being self-deprecating, or by being able to work with the crowd—that is one of the major tasks for the young comic.[15]

Several comics report that, in the beginning, it may take several days or even weeks to recover from a bad set. As one comic describes it:

> It hurts a lot when you bomb, and the hangover can be longer than the eu-

> phoria you feel from the good sets. The hangover is like an assault on your core. It reaffirms all of the self-doubt that you have about yourself—and it can last a long time.

In order to survive, the newcomer must learn strategies to anesthetize himself. Initially, the aspiring comic develops techniques to *manage failure;* later, he learns ways to *avoid* bombing.

<u>Managing Failure: Coping with the Aftermath of "Bombing"</u>

One method comics use to manage "bombing" is to share their feelings with other comics. A simple "They're brutal tonight!" is often enough to elicit an encouraging remark from a fellow comic. One comedienne observes that sometimes they don't even have to speak: "Your eyes meet another comic's and they understand."(8)

Some comics report that they might take a long walk or go for a run after a bad set. Others go home and call a trusted friend if they need to share.(7)

Many comics describe a process of giving themselves a pep talk to work through the depression after bombing. Some of the ways comics encourage themselves include the following:

- I would tell myself, "So what? I'm never going to see these people again."(16)
- Don't be so worried about strangers; just keep getting up there and adding to your laughs.(4)

- I tried to tell myself, "No guts, no glory. The rejection? It only hurts for a little while."[17]

- I thought. "I just have be willing to jump in the water and sink for a while."[3]

- You learn there is nothing fatal. What are they going to do, kill you?[4]

- Eventually, you come to the point where you tell yourself, "I like doing this. This is what I want to do. I just have to power through it."[6]

- I tried to accept that doing stand-up was not going to be easy at first, and that I'm going to have to do it a long time before I get really good. *You have to look at comedy like it's a marathon, not a sprint.*[3]

- You look at yourself in the mirror and tell yourself, "Well, tomorrow is another day," or, you tell yourself, "It's not the first time I've bombed, and it won't be the last. It's all part of the game."[12]

- Whatever your fears are, conquer them. I forced myself to go up every night. Gradually, you are able to hide your fear and then find moments of comfort on stage. I don't think the fear goes away; you just run out of things you haven't seen before.[70]

- I looked at hecklers as a challenge, like it was *the next thing I had to learn to do*. Then, I learned that *you are going to bomb. That's how you get better.*[65]

- You tell yourself, "Look, there are a lot of different variables: you, the audience, the room, the previous performer(s), the night of the week, and the events of the day. *It's not just you.*"

- This business is trial and error. All of the negative things that happen to you make you try harder. Bombing is the only way to get better. This is the only art form that uses every human emotion–even failure.[100]

Comedian Rocky LaPorte adds that it helped him when he saw some big names "tank it," and when he received encouraging feedback from other types of entertainers:

> What really made an impression on me is that I saw some very big people bomb. I just said, "Oh." I saw that it was part of the business. That made bombing a little bit easier for me.
>
> Then, I also met some other big entertainers who told me, "Man, I don't know how you do it. You're up there without a net. If we mess up, we can do a re-take or re-shoot it." Sometimes, when other people point things out to you, you say, "I think they're right."[42]

Some comics indicate that to recover from bombing they tried to reinforce their confidence in their "funny." Comic/mime Lou Adams, for example, explains that:

> You remember that you've made people laugh your whole life. You ac-

> cept that the desire to make people laugh is the bottom line for you and that, for you, there is no sound like laughter. ... Remembering that helps motivate you so that even when you've had a bad set, you can come back.[19]

Finally, Diane Nichols sums up some advice that was echoed by other comics:

> I feel like going up to the ones who are visibly shaking, touching them on the shoulder, and telling them, "Look, nobody is going to shoot you. They're probably not even going to remember that you bombed. They're not at home making voodoo dolls of you, you know."
>
> It's important to realize that no matter how bad you are, it's okay. You can come back and do it again. ... Don't judge your progress by anybody else. If you really want to be a stand-up, and you've made people laugh all your life, and you get some laughs, keep doing it. You, and only you, decide whether to keep going.
>
> It's important to realize that it is *not* going to be easy, and just relax behind that attitude. And, you can't take things too personally, because the audience doesn't. They can love you for an hour, and then they won't

> even remember your name five minutes into the parking lot.[4]

The messages above make the pain easier to endure until the comic can become desensitized—and more proficient. Eventually, the comic reaches a point where he begins to believe that he is funny *even though he may bomb*. Comic John Wing describes that moment of confidence this way:

> There'll come a night when you'll bomb. You'll do terribly, and they'll hate you. And, after that show, you'll realize that they were wrong. Once you realize that, you'll be okay. You'll say, "F—k them. I'm funnier than they think."[28]

Learning Techniques to Avoid Failure

At the amateur stage, aspiring comics also begin to learn specific techniques to avoid failure. For instance, many comics begin to record their sets to see what material made the audience laugh. Recording also allows them to see at what point in the joke the laugh falls, and it helps them analyze what they could do better. Reviewing the recording permits the comic to think of a new reference for a joke, incorporate something funny from an audience interaction, or add something they had not considered.

Comic Nick Gaza describes the process he uses to evaluate new jokes:

> When I listen to the new jokes, I ask myself: "Am I performing the joke the way I heard it in my head when I

> thought of the joke? Did I do the joke justice?"[46]

Steve Altman reports that recording his set allows him to capture things that happen "off the cuff." He states:

> Taping also allows you to catch something you did that was totally spontaneous and in the moment. Later you'll go, "What was that thing I did?" and you may not recall it. Then, you review the recording, write it down, and you can expand it. It also gives you the confidence that you *can* go off the script in the middle of the show and come up with something good.[51]

To avoid failing, many comics review their new material immediately before going on stage to be certain that they have a new joke memorized. In addition, a smart amateur will also pre-edit his material. As one comic describes it:

> You go over new material one more time. You judge it critically before performing it. You ask yourself, "Will this be as funny as it was at home?"

Several comics recommend that the newcomer know what material he is going to do, and then rehearse the presentation of those jokes. Comic Fritz Coleman explains the importance of practicing one's material:

> You can have a piece of material that is wonderful, but if you are not used to saying the words over and over,

> then you deliver it in a wary fashion. You don't deliver it with gusto, and so people don't buy it. But, as soon as you've said the words over and over and slam them right out there, and it's part of the flow of your set, then people buy it and it becomes funny. Then, it really is a funny piece of material.

Actively watching other comics also plays a part in learning to improve one's performance. The comic-in-training can learn how the masters handle difficult situations, as well as observe the mistakes others make. To paraphrase one comic, "It's all up there for you to see, if you choose to learn." However, as one cocktail waitress/aspiring comic cautions, "There is nothing like actually getting up and performing." Comic Chris Clobber adds that the young comic must also learn how to control the silence *as well as the laughter.*[(100)]

Using a successful set as a reference point is another technique comics cite as a way to avoid bombing. As one comic put it, "You search for whatever was there that worked so you can start to do that consistently." Another comic adds, "If you are smart, you will take note of the things that get laughs and begin to build on those."

Finally, Jim Shubert recommends that the amateur should do a "critical retrospective of the performance." He explains:

> You'll ask yourself, "What could I have done differently? What did I do that made them restless? Where did I lose

> them? If it happens again, what can I do to make things better?"[3]

Learning Basic Performing Skills

Many amateurs must learn the basics of performing from scratch. Comedian Jimmy Brogan, former head writer on *The Tonight Show*, describes such an experience:

> The first time I got up there, I didn't even know how to adjust the microphone. I just sort of left it low and bent over. And, I didn't know the lights were going to be so bright. You couldn't see anybody. It's hundreds of shows before you get comfortable up there. You can't really be comfortable enough to be yourself when you start, because you don't even know what to do with your hands.[40]

One of the most basic things the amateur learns is how to handle a microphone in a way that conveys a professional demeanor. Comic Ron Richards provides an example:

> I used to leave the microphone in the stand and just talked, which is good if you want to work on television because you get used to working like a host with a boom mic overhead. But, the trouble was that being a tall guy, I ended up stooping over. I also had a tendency to grab the mic stand and fling it this way and that way. Then, it

> was in between my legs, and I thought, "That's too sloppy." Then, I started doing the most common thing for comics, where I took the microphone out of its stand. I'd seen other guys say, "Hi, how are you?" and remove the microphone from the stand, then set the mic stand over to the side. So, I did that.
>
> But, new people are funny. I saw one woman who was short. She did not adjust the microphone stand. She just bent the microphone down and talked up at it. It looked like she was talking up to her showerhead. You forget how new everything is when people have never been on stage before.[25]

It should be noted that while removing the microphone from its stand is the most common technique, the comic may work in ways that best fit his style once he is past the basics.

Learning Stage Etiquette

The aspiring comic also learns the basic elements of stage etiquette at the amateur phase. Proper stage demeanor includes such things as shaking hands with the comic who has just introduced you, greeting the audience, and ending your set when you get the "red light" that indicates the end of your stage time. Expected behavior also includes encouraging the crowd to tip the cocktail staff and acknowledging the sound technician or piano player for doing a good job. Finally, proper stage etiquette includes thanking the audience and introducing the next comic. Stating the next comic's performing credits helps to keep the show moving and it encourages the audience to pay attention to the next performer.

<u>Putting Your First Ten Minutes of Material Together</u>

At the same time the amateur comic is working to overcome his fear and learn basic performing skills, he must begin to develop material. For a significant portion of his first year, the aspiring comic is accumulating his first few minutes of jokes.

Some comics report that when they started, they did jokes from joke books or they used old jokes they knew. Other comics strung together the jokes that got laughs each week as they went on stage and they built their first few minutes by keeping what worked.

Some amateurs pay other comics to help them develop material. However, like the following comedienne, most newcomers discover that, ultimately, there are few shortcuts:

> I went to some of the guys who zero in on someone new, convince you they're a writer and get you to pay them. ... I was poor, but I put aside $50, which, to me, was like $5,000. I paid somebody to sit with me and basically write everything myself. Then, I found out that I can't have anyone write for me. It is not funny when you are not being yourself.[20]

As they create their early material, most comics struggle to find *that which will make audiences laugh* and *that which is funny about themselves*—and then they hang on to whatever worked. However, several comedians also suggest that the amateur should work on putting together a segment of jokes that work. As Tom Ryan describes it:

> Hone five minutes of material that works. Don't try new material every night. Get some jokes to where they work. Get the *rhythm and the feel* of five minutes that works.[64]

Eventually, the amateur-level comic learns to let the audience guide him, and he continues to refine the process of "building minutes" over the next several years.

<u>Developing Stage Comfort</u>

After approximately one year of performing regularly at "open mic" nights, the typical newcomer begins to develop greater ease on stage. One comedienne describes the essence of stage comfort this way:

> I never had any confidence in myself, and that's why it's taken me all this time to get up there and smile and just be with everyone, and not separate myself like I was less than them or not as funny as the other comics. Somehow, that all passed. Now, when I am on stage, it's my space no matter where I am. I get on stage, and I feel the lights on me, and I look out, and I'm okay. I know what I do, and ninety-nine percent of the time when I get up there, I'm glad to be there.[8]

Another comic describes the process of developing stage presence as follows:

> You move from *not being sure* you belong on stage to *acting as though* you belong on stage, to *knowing* you belong on stage.[4]

Like getting past one's fear and coping with rejection, developing stage presence is an individual process. For those comics who are stronger *writers* than performers, becoming comfortable on stage may take several years. For comics who are *strong on personality to begin with*, developing ease on stage can take less than a year.

Jimmy Burns suggests that developing stage presence is "something that you may not even know you are learning and that there are no rules for learning it." He adds, "It's a confidence that comes from going up on stage regularly, over time."[39]

Beginning to Interact with Audiences

Learning to interact with audiences is another skill that the amateur must master during the first year or two. However, there was considerable variation among comics with respect to the ease they felt in interacting with audiences. For some comics, talking to the audience is very difficult in the beginning. Comedienne Diane Nichols recalls:

> Learning to talk to the audience is a big thing, and it's very hard for some of us. In the beginning, I couldn't even stand up. My legs would shake so badly that I would sit. One day,

> a comic friend of mine just looked at me and in the sweetest possible voice said, "Diane, tonight stand the f--k up." I did, and I haven't sat down again. But, the first time I could talk to the crowd was important because that can save you. Just being able to play along and get a laugh out of the audience is important. When you reach that plateau, that's a great year for you because then you can handle yourself.(4)

For the more outgoing comics, talking with audiences is a relatively easy skill to master. In fact, "partying with audiences" can come so naturally for some, that newer comics may rely on it too much in the beginning to the exclusion of mastering the technical aspects of writing and performing.(12)

Showcasing

After performing at "open mic" nights for about one year, the amateur is likely to have evolved into one of the funnier "open mic" performers. He will have developed some degree of stage presence and will have built up enough material to showcase for a club owner or talent booker.

Auditioning for a club owner may mean performing five or ten minutes of material for the owner. If the set goes well, the comic may be hired or placed on the owner's active list of prospective performers. If the owner starts to give the comic paid spots, the comic is in the ideal position: he is getting paid, and he is getting the stage time he needs to develop. However, at the better clubs, getting scheduled for stage time is competitive, and breaking into the paying spots can be arbitrary because showcasing and scheduling decisions are often at the owner's discretion. A comic may have to audition several times before he is hired.

Young performers who are not ready for paid performing spots may be encouraged to hang out and pick up what they can by watching the other comics. After a few months, they may showcase again to achieve paid performer status. Alternately, an owner may see the comic perform, decide they are ready, and move them to the list of paid performers.

The comics report that club owners look for a variety of things when they assess new talent. Some club owners look for an individual who has *the potential to be good* or *the potential to be a star*. Many owners look for someone who has a well-defined comic attitude, an unusual character, or someone who has strong stage presence. Some owners will look for something they think they can help the comic develop.(5) This "something" may be a line or a character that the club owner feels the comic can build off of.(5) Some club owners take pride in nurturing new talent and giving young talent an opportunity to develop.

Many owners look for someone they believe will be a good fit with their patrons or someone who will do a solid job for them on a busy weekend. Some owners will look for a comic who can be a good "second banana." Like the players who sit on the bench in baseball, such comics fill a necessary role: not only can they do an adequate job in an evening's line-up, but it allows audiences to know who the good comics are.

Moving from "Open Mic" to Opening Act

After eight or twelve months of performing at "open mic" nights, the amateur typically reaches his first major plateau. As one comic describes it, "You get to feeling good about yourself because, as 'open mic' guys go, you are doing good." Several comics indicate that the amateur reaches this step at the point when he is no longer paralyzed by fear or when he begins interacting with the crowd. Other comics report that the amateur reaches this plateau when he has developed his first fifteen to twenty minutes of material. The latter is a significant achievement because it can take up to a year and a half to build a decent twenty minutes, showcase successfully, and secure work as an opening act.

The transition to opening act is an interesting event among comics. Several comics report that they knew precisely when they had hit this plateau. Comic Jim Shubert states that he "felt it within himself when he was ready for the next step up." Shubert provides the following example of a transition from the amateur phase to the opening act stage:

> I felt myself hit the plateaus. I remember one Monday night, I was working a day job and I got up at eight a.m. to go to work. I'd get off work at six p.m., and I'd have to drive directly from my day job all the way across town to a club. You sign the list. They put you on. I did a set there. I recorded it. Boom, I ran right out of there after I got off stage. I jumped in my car and drove across town to another club in Westwood. I did an-

> other fifteen-minute set and tried out some new jokes. Boom, I ran down to another bistro in Culver City. They got to know me there and they'd put me on stage. Then I'd come back to a club in Los Angeles at midnight, and get a fourth set. The first time I did that I felt myself hit a plateau where I said, "I'm not an 'open mic' comic any more."(3)

Finding a Mentor

As the amateur approaches the end of the "open mic" phase, he or she may set about finding a mentor. The process of finding someone who will "teach you the ropes" and/or vouch for you includes hanging out at the better clubs and getting to know veteran comics, bookers, and club owners.

A veteran comic may be willing to help younger comics for a number of reasons that range from kindness to self-interest. First, some comics are good people who are willing to go out of their way to help others. Second, the veteran comic may see something of himself in the novice. They may feel empathy for those starting out, or they may feel adamantly about young talent not making the same mistakes they made. Third, the older comic may dislike those in the business who exploit others and want to protect the younger comic from predators. Fourth, giving a younger comic a break may occur because the veteran and the amateur have the right chemistry. For example, a veteran comic may invite a younger comic to open for him because the younger comic is someone with whom the older comic can hang out comfortably while working on the road.

Finally, helping a young comic is also a matter of enlightened self-interest for the veteran. If younger comics "come up in the wrong way" and become mediocre performers, it will ultimately take money out of the older comic's pocket. For example, if the public says, "Yes, I went to the comedy club, but the comics weren't very good," then the loss of club business will hurt the older comic's livelihood. Without business, clubs close. Thus, the veteran comedian has a vested interest in seeing that those coming up learn the craft properly. *Veteran performers serve as gatekeepers who protect the industry by screening out poor talent and by mentoring young comics who will make people laugh.*

Comedy writer Jarrod Cardwell recommends that the amateur should "get in and get out of the 'open mic' scene." Cardwell observes:

> Comics who have been bad for three to five years, don't "get it." Either they don't care, or they lack the talent. They don't have the aesthetic for what a good comic is or what a good joke is. You either "get it" (i.e., what makes people laugh and what is funny) or you don't. Those people who don't "get it," don't become great professional comics. People who "get it," learn quickly. Smart people start clustering and help each other. The unfunny people also cluster and can languish at the "open mic" phase for years.[45]

Cardwell suggests using the open microphone nights *to gain the necessary experience* and *to make contacts*. He recommends this strategy as a transition to the opening act stage because:

> Professional comics will tell the newcomer exactly what to do and point him or her in the right direction. On the other hand, newcomers may learn bad habits from other amateurs and, thereby, stagnate.[45]

Cardwell notes that many young performers who make it into the larger clubs today make friends with a "bigger" comic who gives them an opening spot; alternately, some amateurs decide to actively come into contact with a comedy club system.[71]

If a comic has already apprenticed elsewhere and has come to the industry centers of Los Angeles or New York with some experience, Cardwell recommends not getting bogged down in the "open mic" scene. If the comic has amateur experience, he or she is more likely to stand out as being "ahead of the curve." If such a comic hangs out at the better clubs and demonstrates talent, he is likely to find someone who will say, "Yes, this person is funny. He has what it takes."

Getting the First Paying Jobs

At eight to twelve months, many comics report that they got their first paying job. The early "paid gigs" for the comics were small bars, café's, coffee houses, and bowling alleys. As one comic put it, "You go on anywhere they are willing to pay you." Typically, the amount they were paid was small, ranging from $5 to $10 per set to $40 for the weekend. One comic recalled being paid in *change*.

The first paying job is significant for the amateur because being paid symbolizes "progress" and it encourages the comic's professional aspirations. Comic Paul Dillery, for example, recalls that when he started to be paid, he thought, "Well, I must be on the right track."

At this point, an enterprising newcomer will also begin to ask around, make calls, and actively begin to learn about the different places there are to work. If he has accumulated enough material to open, he is now poised to work as an Opening Act.

Some "Food for Thought" for the Aspiring Comic

At the same time veteran comics offer help to talented newcomers, they also have sobering words of caution for aspiring comics. Relatively few comedians would actively encourage an amateur to go into stand-up comedy. Working comics offer the following "advice" to the would-be comic:

- I would tell them to try walking into a fan first. If they can survive that, then I would tell them they have a chance at best.(30)

- Go into real estate. Save your sanity. Mama's don't let your babies grow up to be stand-ups. Talent burns a high octane.(17)

- You have to be willing to take the beating. You are going to have nights when the audience doesn't like you. If you can't take that rejection, become an agent.(52)

- Making it is partly talent, partly luck, partly your own ambition, and partly being in the right place at the right time with the right stuff. This business is a roll of the dice.[30]

- Remember, five minutes is an eternity if you are not funny. (Source: Steve Landesberg, courtesy of Joey Gaynor)[52]

- If you are not funny by the time you are twelve, don't even think about doing comedy professionally. (Source: Steve Allen, courtesy of Charlie Hill)[33]

- If you absolutely have to do stand-up or there will be an empty space in your life, then do it, because you will never be a whole human being. But, if you don't need to do it to be contented, stay the hell out because it will cut you to pieces. It will chew you up.

  If that is the happiest you are in life when you are up there, then you have to do it, because for those few moments that is the essence of life. It's why God put you on earth.

  If you only get the feeling of being in tune with life and of being connected to the universe when you are on stage, then that's the place you've got to be. If it doesn't really matter to you, then don't do it—because you are not really meant to do it. If you get that feeling from anything else, do that instead.[30]

Comedian Rudy Moreno adds that the "open mic" and the opening act phases are *not* a punishment—they exist for the young comic's long-term benefit. Moreno explains:

> There are many young people who think they are going to walk in and be discovered. They think someone is going to walk up and say, "Hey kid, I'm going to make you a star." Well, that isn't going to happen.
>
> There are also a lot of guys now who get on stage in a main room on an off-night and think they've made it. They think they *should* be up there with the headliners and the middlers. That's not true—because you have to pay your dues. That's how the chain works. The "open mic" and opening act stages are there for your own learning process. That is where you get the experience you will *need* in order to do this job.
>
> Don't try to go from "step one" to "step eight." It *will* backfire on you. And when it does, you will start doubting yourself. You will have no confidence, *and* you won't have the experience on stage to back it up.[43]

Comedian John Caparulo offers the following suggestions for "open mic" comics:

> Just... be... funny. If you are funny, you will get noticed. Also, take each step in turn. Develop three good minutes so that they will give you five. Then, work on five solid minutes so they give

> you seven—and then ten. Finally, just because you *think* you have some "chunks" of material, that doesn't mean that it's all good, or that it all fits together.[71]

Finally, Bob Fisher, owner of the Ice House Comedy Club, adds the following dose of reality for would-be comedians:

> Comedy absolutely has to be in your heart; the odds are so slim of making it. There are no "overnight successes." You spend a minimum of twelve years working the clubs before you even get that one-in-a-million shot at stardom. The longer I am in this business, the higher the percentage that I attribute to luck. Now, I would say that making it is 65 percent luck and 35 percent talent. A comic can work hard and be good, and he or she will still need that big break that comes from knowing someone or being what somebody happens to be looking for at that moment.

Barbara's "Take" on the Amateur Phase

The aspiring comic should be aware that a career in comedy involves a difficult apprenticeship. Do it if you are driven and have made people laugh, but know that learning the craft requires courage, hard work, and perseverance. The performing skills and grace under pressure required by the craft take time to develop. Finding your "funny," learning to write, and translating your material on the stage *will* take several years. Then comes the struggle to make a living doing comedy. The applause is rewarding and the work offers a wonderful creative outlet. However, this performing art has a high price tag: it is emotionally difficult and carries no guarantee of stardom.

SOME ESSENTIALS FOR MAKING IT

- Be extremely focused and extremely driven. You must say, "This is what I want to do," and then pursue it aggressively.[6]
- Remember that there is no substitute for good taste.[64]
- Keep it all in the spirit of fun; nobody gets hurt.[64]
- Have a "hook"; something about you that is completely different than anybody else.[53]
- Observe the masters, the true geniuses, and learn — but also remember to be yourself.[61]
- I think the key to success is optimism, obsession with your goals, and holding to your obligations. You can't be a flake.[48]
- Learn about the business aspects of this job. Make your business skills a strength. Develop a strong entrepreneurial spirit.[39]
- Know your strength and play to it. If you write well, write; then, team up with another comic who can book gigs well, or someone who can close well—even with a tough audience. Not enough comics work together.[4]
- Respect the audience. They're the boss. Your job is to go out and make them have a good time so they come back to the club—and so they come to see you again. If you want to juggle, play guitar, or stick a message in there, that's fine; but make them laugh. That's the job.[69]

AT EVERY LEVEL THERE ARE STAGES

First, you're a beginning amateur.
Then, with practice, you get to be
one of the better amateurs.

Next, you are a beginning opening act.
Then, after a while, you become a
seasoned opener.

Then, you are a beginning feature act.
And, gradually, you develop into a very
good feature act.

Finally, you become a beginning headliner.
Then, you work your way up into being an
experienced headliner.

Then, there are exceptional comedians
who are not just club headliners. They are
beyond "club comic." They're the guys
who attain "star" status.

– Joey Medina

CHAPTER 4

THE OPENING ACT PHASE: YEARS 1 – 3
GETTING THE MAJOR PIECES TO WORK TOGETHER

AH, YES, THE EARLY YEARS

Two Shows—for the Price of One?

One time, early in my career, I got a gig at a pizza place, but I was literally performing in a doorway that was in between two different rooms. The two audiences didn't see each other because they were in two separate rooms. I got through the show; but afterward, I asked the manager, "Am I going to get paid double for this?"

- Andres Fernandez

But, I Was Just Trying to Help! Or Was I?

I had been doing stand-up for a year or so, and I had hooked up with a group called Clean Comedians. They sent me to do a gig at a church. It was Sunday morning and I went up to perform during Sunday service. So, I started telling my jokes. Now, I'm a black kid and this was a white, conservative church, so that made things interesting enough. But then, there was an older lady with purple hair who was sitting at the organ. Every time that I got to the punch line of a joke, she would play these same chords on the organ. I guess it was her idea of, like, doing a "drum roll" after a joke to emphasize the punch line. But, she kept doing it after *every single joke*. Maybe she was upset that I was taking some of her music time away, or maybe she didn't think doing comedy in church was appropriate, I don't know. I kept trying to give her the high sign not to do that anymore, and somehow she kept turning away from me in between the jokes. So, there I am, dying up there, and I'm thinking, "Lady, you are not helping. Do you *want* me to die here?"

- Willis Turner

Sound and Lighting? Nah!

I once performed at an Indian reservation where they actually put the cars in a circle, and they all had their headlights on in order to light my performance. It was awful.

Another time, I performed at a hockey game, and the microphone cord was run through the glass partition that protects people from getting hit by hockey pucks. But, the microphone cord only extended out for about six feet. Now, I tend to move around on stage. I kept trying to pull on the cord, and the sound system kept echoing the jokes.

- Charlie Hill

The Sacrificial Lamb

When you are opening you are a sacrificial lamb. You're thrown to the wolves. You're breaking the group in. You're calming them down. You're letting them know they are an *audience*. You're setting the whole tone for the evening. It's tough, but you learn a lot. You learn how to break a crowd when it's ice cold. And, you learn how to get a crowd when there are only ten people in the audience.

- John Caponera

CHAPTER 4

THE OPENING ACT PHASE: YEARS 1–3
GETTING THE MAJOR PIECES TO WORK TOGETHER

Openers? We are the front line; the Marines
of show business. We land first. We clear the turf
for the headliner. We make them an audience.
We make the beach landable.
Tim Jones

Overview of the Opening Act Phase

During the second and third years of performing, the young comic typically begins to work as an opening act. In "headline clubs" that feature a three-act show (i.e., an opening act, a middle act, and a headline act), the opening act opens the show and performs for fifteen minutes. The opening act's job is to gain the audience's focus, to warm them up, and to get them listening and laughing as a group.

It is as an opening act that the young comedian becomes exposed to all of the basic components of stand-up comedy. During this period, the young comic begins the long process of "finding himself" as a humorist. He gradually builds a solid core of effective material and begins to develop consistency as a performer. In addition, the comic is learning a great deal about different audiences and different performing venues.

At this stage, the comic also learns to serve as a master of ceremonies, and he learns how to make a living doing comedy. The Opening Act phase has been called "an investment" that provides the necessary preparation for the young comic to work on the road—where additional seasoning and more money are to be found.[61]

Finally, as comic John Caponera points out, "Opening act is the point where you begin having fun on stage, and you start getting some of the rewards from your work."

What Happens During the Opening Act Phase

The major skills and experiences of the Opening Act phase are:

- Getting to know your comic voice
- Learning to write comedy
- Learning to weather dry spells and plateaus
- Learning about timing, delivery, and other performing techniques
- Beginning to interact with audiences
- Learning the role of master of ceremonies
- Learning to handle hecklers and other interruptions
- Noticing more about one's surroundings and learning about different venues
- Learning about the properties of energy in a room
- Learning about diverse audiences
- Learning to make a living at comedy

- Starting to have fun with stand-up
- Transitioning to the feature act stage

Getting to Know Your Comic Voice

During the first two or three years of performing, the young comic is confronted with many questions as he searches for his own unique comic voice: Do I want to tell jokes? Do I want to tell stories? Do I want to stand still? Do I want to move around? Do I want to *say funny things* or do I want to *say things funny*? Do I want to do political humor, shock comedy, observational humor, or insult humor? Do I want to use props? Do I want to be zany, deadpan, sarcastic, or naïve? Do I want to do improvisational comedy or impressions? With all of these choices, it is not surprising that the comic may experiment with different styles during the opening act phase. Kevin Jordan recalls:

> In the beginning, I was like a rudderless ship. I was funny, but I hadn't developed a comic voice on stage. I tried to be real "blue," but it didn't work for me. I tried song parodies, and that didn't work for me. Next, I tried props—and that wasn't me. Then, as a feature act, I finally found my voice in comedy.[54]

Comic Eddie Merrill further observes, "When you first start out, you are often borrowing from a lot of different styles." Merrill adds:

> I don't know of anybody who starts out and, wham, they're a unique

> character. The young comic may have the nucleus of that character; but, they have to develop it to a point where other people are aware of it. Even Emo Philips, Bobcat Goldthwaite, and Sam Kinison went through a dozen incarnations. So, you start out not necessarily doing other people's jokes, but you may borrow their mannerisms or styles until you find yourself.[21]

The comics report that as an opening act, the young comedian is still learning what it is about him that works with audiences. As comic John Caponera notes:

> Eventually you develop a style and a persona, but you don't discover that until a couple of years in the business.[21]

John Wing adds:

> For the first two or three years, you go up with a different attitude and feeling a different way. In the beginning, you are just not sure they are going to laugh.[28]

By using audiences as a "looking glass," the comic gradually learns *how audiences see him* and *what audiences find funny and endearing about him*.[22] In time, the comic comes to understand which of his attitudes or attributes consistently produces laughs. He then begins to focus on those parts of himself when he writes new material.

Several comics state that one aspect of finding their comic persona involved *proving to themselves that they were funny*. John Caponera, for example, describes the process he went through in finding himself as a young comic:

> The big challenge for me was proving to myself that I could be funny without having to do a voice or imitating somebody else's personality. I had to prove that my personality was funny and that I could be funny being myself.(13)

For some comics, "growth" in their persona included giving up props (e.g., a funny hat, funny glasses, or a rubber chicken, etc.). As comic Eddie Merrill explains:

> I started out doing straight stand-up, then I changed to doing prop comedy because I could get more material from the props. But the more props I had, the harder it got to go from gig to gig. So, eventually I said, "I'm going to 86 all of them." I found out that it was psychological. I was just using the props to hide behind because I hadn't found my character. I hadn't found *myself*.
>
> It took an experience in front of a concert-size crowd for me to learn that it was personality that was important. *It was your character on stage and how much the audience liked that character* that was important. After

> that, you can pretty much do and say whatever you find funny through your character.[21]

Some comics recall that the process of "finding themselves" involved watching other comics. Comic Paul Dillery, for example, notes that, "Watching the competition and seeing what everyone else did inspired me to try to be different and unique."[24]

Observing other comedians often helps the young comic to identify what he likes or dislikes on stage. Comic Ron Richards explains:

> It takes a while to figure out what you like about someone because you just like them. You don't know whether it's because they stand still or move around on stage, or whatever. However, when people do something that really bothers you, you can put your finger on it right away, like if they yell or if they are rude.[25]

Although watching other comics often serves an important function, the comedian's growth process also includes a gradual realization by the young comic that he needs to *be himself* rather than to imitate others. One comedienne, for example, observes that at about the two-year mark:

> You start learning that comedy comes from within and that you can't "do" someone else. You have to be you. Then, you start to form an opinion of what you want your comedy to be.[26]

John Caponera agrees that eventually the rookie learns that he must be himself:

> You can't copy another comic because you are only cheating yourself. What makes you funny is you, and your point of view. By imitating someone else, you're not being true to yourself or the audience.[13]

Interestingly, several comics report that this element of a rookie's professional growth was noticeable to his fellow comics. Moreover, veterans will offer the novice a supportive word when they notice his progress. As comic John Caponera observes:

> You can always see when a comic has come into his own. You see someone starting out doing stock material and even doing other people's expressions and mannerisms. Then, one day, he's decided to chuck it and really be himself, and you say, "Wow, he's really become his own comic."[13]

Another dimension of a comic "getting to know himself" is learning what his image on-stage *should* be. As comic John Wing describes it:

> In the beginning, you don't know how to dress, you don't have any idea of how you look on stage, and you don't have any idea of how you *should* look on stage.[28]

During this phase, the rookie becomes aware that his image on stage can be an important tool for instantly communicating to the audience. For example, the young comic learns that even before he says anything, the audience is scrutinizing him. As one comic describes it, "While you are walking up, the audience is already asking themselves, 'What is going to be funny about this person?'"[13]

In the following excerpt, comedian John Caponera explains how important it is for the comic to structure his first few minutes on stage:

> Your first two minutes on stage are so critical. You're letting the audience know so much. They're sizing you up. They're figuring you out. You have to let them like you before you can do anything funny. Your objective is to get them on your side. You are greeting them. You are welcoming them, and letting them get used to the sound of your voice. Then, if they like you, they will give you the benefit of the doubt with the material.[13]

The young comic also learns to use his physical characteristics as the basis for material.[5] For some comics, presenting an image that is consistent with their physical appearance and personality is easily resolved. Being bald or ethnic, very tall or short, fat or skinny, etc., immediately conveys a certain image to the audience. In addition, comics who dress or behave eccentrically on stage or who come from an identifiable region of the country have easily identifiable "hooks" (i.e., a way for the audience to remember the comic).

For other comics, however, it can take several years to determine what is funny about them and what appearance is most consistent with their personality. As comedienne Diane Nichols describes it:

> I don't have a natural built-in gimmick like someone who comes from an ethnic background or has a different body build. There are some of us who are really like your next-door neighbor. I'm like the receptionist in your office. In fact, that's been my biggest problem as far as the industry goes; they have wanted me to be immediately identified as something.[(4)]

In addition, there is often comic fodder in "playing against type," and it can take time to learn whether that is appropriate. For example, Henry Cho is a Korean American comedian from Tennessee who has a Southern accent, and there are several jokes in his act that emphasize this and "play against" what you might expect at first glance.

As he gets to know his image, the young comic often begins to incorporate the old vaudeville advice, "Do a few jokes on yourself, up-front." Doing several jokes about a prominent physical feature at the beginning of the comic's set serves several functions. First, self-deprecation puts the audience at ease.[(5)] Second, commenting on an obvious feature acknowledges to the audience that the comic understands how he comes across to them.[(5)] Third, "If the comic makes fun of himself early on, it disarms the heckler."[(5)]

Female comics must confront several other issues with respect to "image." Some comediennes have chosen to be "super feminine" while others have elected to be "ultra self-deprecating." As one comedienne describes it, "Those are two spheres that are not competitive in the male sense." Another struggle for some comediennes is whether or not to emphasize their appearance. Karen Babbitt explains:

> For a while, I'd have managers who'd give me different ways that they wanted me to hold the microphone or ways that I should have my hair. They'd say, "Try to play your looks up." "Try to play your looks down." "Wear a dress." "Cover your breasts." They gave me all kinds of different tacks; and, what happened is that I really got into writing comedy.[20]

Although the timetable may vary, when the young comic *begins to identify his "image"* and *no longer imitates other comics* he has taken two major steps on the road to finding his own comic signature. He also has mastered two crucial tasks associated with moving from opening act to middle act status.

Learning to Write Comedy

When they start, most young comics do not have a clear understanding of what writing for the craft entails. During the second and third years, they must learn how to write for the art form. As one comic observes:

> In the beginning, it's like, "I just want to say what I want to say. I want to be liked. I want people to agree with me, and I want them to laugh at the same

> things I laugh at"—then comes the process of becoming a comedian.[10]

Some rookies start out working "dirty." Material that is profane or vulgar is easier to do when the comic doesn't know how to write comedy. The young comic finds that people will respond to a poor, but dirty, joke with nervous laughter. Given the prospect of bombing, getting some reaction from dirty material is easier for many novices than "dying" with clean but unpolished material.

As they learn to write, many comics draw on the comedy masters they had been exposed to while growing up. Comic Paul Dillery, for example, suggests that a good way of learning to write is to see the routines of comedy masters printed out and then study the way jokes or routines are written. Dillery explains:

> I read all the books I could about comedy, including comedy writing books. If you are serious, you can go to the library. Get all the old joke books and listen to comedy recordings [e.g., CDs, records, and DVDs]. That's how you learn. I still do that every once in a while for inspiration.[24]

The comics state that by experimenting, you find out what you prefer and what you do well (e.g., telling stories or one-liners), and you begin to learn how to put a good joke together. However, the young comic also learns that a "good written joke" represents hard work.

One of the first things the comic learns about constructing a good written joke is that his material must be very clear. As one comic explains, "You have to tell the audience where you are going, and you have to be very specific about it."[39] In addition, the ideas the comic uses should be general enough for most people to understand. The comic's goal is to reach as many people in the audience as possible. Comic John Roarke sums up the importance of learning to communicate your ideas clearly as follows:

> As a comedian, you are attempting to communicate truth so that other people can understand it. It is communication, and you know it when you feel that you and the audience are one, culminated by laughter. Whether you have this experience earlier or later in your career, the more you can recreate it, the more proficient you can say you are as a comedian.[27]

The young comic also learns that "brevity is the soul of wit," and that he should craft jokes "in the fewest possible words."[28] As comic Paul Dillery explains:

> The main thing is just to be concise. That is where newcomers are always having problems. They use too many words. The way to do it is to figure it out on paper. Take the shortest distance between points A and B (your set up and punch line). Get to the funny part as quickly as you can.[24]

Comedian Steve McGrew agrees and describes the importance of being concise this way:

> If you have *two more beats* in a joke than is necessary, it's not funny. Comedy has a rhythm and a meter to it. You have to learn that. That is a key part of learning to write for the craft.[44]

Paul Dillery further observes that as the young comic learns to write, he also learns little "tricks of the trade" such as using sharp nouns and strong consonants. Dillery explains:

> You learn to use sharp words. It's true that the K sound is funny—that Ks are funnier than some other letters. Remember the scene in the *Sunshine Boys* when they were going, "Carrot is funnier than lima bean." Cs are funny, Ks are funny.[24]

In addition, the rookie also learns the basics of joke structure. For example, the comic learns techniques such as putting the key word at the end of the joke. The novice also learns the value of using opposites in the set-up and the punch line. As one comic describes it:

> I look at joke structure in terms of opposites. You set up in the first part of the joke the exact opposite of what you payoff in the punch line. It's creating an incongruity, or something that's a surprise from what you had set up.[27]

In addition to such basic writing techniques, the comic learns to draw on all of his experiences for material. For example, the comic might use the experience of having a broken leg or performing with a marching band for material, or he may draw on early childhood experiences for a joke.

As he learns to write, the comic must also train himself to see humor around him. In essence, the young comic is *learning to find humor in any situation*. He is honing the skill of *making things funny* so that this becomes a tool at his command on stage.

Many comics report that at this stage they began to devote a certain amount of time to writing during the day. Observational comics often look through newspapers and magazines for inspiration.[17] As comedian Ron Richards points out:

> Whatever sparks you is good. The important thing is that, "Good Fortune follows Righteous Persistence." If you sit down and say, "I'm going to write now," and you work on it, even if you come up with nothing for an hour, ten minutes later in the shower something just goes "boing." If you do the work, then the sudden inspiration while you are walking down the street will come to you because you have trained your mind to look for the comedy.[25]

Rocky LaPorte agrees and states, "Once you get into the habit of sitting down to write, you'll start getting little gems; then, you just cut the fat and work with them on stage."[42]

There are comics, however, who state that they find it difficult to be disciplined about writing. One comic argues that he creates best under improvisational circumstances.[29] Several insist that they must experience something funny or that the humor has to emerge naturally from a funny situation. Still other comics find that it is very useful to develop material by working on material with friends who share a similar sense of humor. Comic Rocky LaPorte states that his writing also has to do with his moods:

> There was a time a few years ago when I was going through a tough time and I couldn't write funny to save my life. Now, I am having fun again. When I am in a good mood, funny stuff just comes to me. I just think funny. You see the absurdity in things or you talk to people and they'll say something silly.[42]

In general, the comics state that the creative process is an individual one, and that the rookie ultimately has to discover the writing process that works best for him.

Regardless of how they develop their jokes, comics at the opening act stage all are concerned with accumulating enough material to become a middle act. To this end, the young comic learns to carry a note pad or recording device with him at all times so that he will be prepared if he thinks of something or observes something funny. As one comic describes it, "As desperate as you are for material, you want to make sure that you don't forget something that you can work into a routine." Veteran comic Tom Ryan adds: "To this day, I feel naked if I don't have a pen with me."[64]

Adding New Material to Your Act

During the opening act stage, the comic must learn how to add jokes to his existing material. One way to add material is by creating "tag lines" for existing jokes. Tag lines are funny lines that are "tagged onto" a previous joke. Tag lines serve to extend the humorous thought and help the comic to sustain laughter.

The novice also learns the value of other techniques such as adding "savers" i.e., funny lines that are inserted after jokes that fail. "Savers" include lines such as:

- Well, that's the last time you'll hear me do *that* joke in public.
- I knew that joke was marginal; but I throw them all out there so you can pick and choose whatever you like. (Johnny Carson)
- Someday you'll be driving home in a car and you'll laugh at that joke, only I won't be there to hear you laugh.[34] (Yakov Smirnov)
- Can everybody hear me okay? These are the jokes, folks!

In addition to adding tag lines to existing jokes, the rookie comic must also learn how to weave new material into his act. Some comics report that they sit down with their material to figure out where the new jokes logically fit. One comic compared this process to a jigsaw puzzle.[28] Other comics state that this process happens by inspiration. For example, one comedienne describes an instinctive process this way:

> What is amazing is that I'll have three jokes that go together, and I'll think of another joke, and I'll be trying to think of where it fits in, and all of a sudden, I'll go, "Oh, there's the obvious place for it. It fits in perfectly." And, I didn't think of it when I wrote the joke. It's sort of like, "what the mind does makes sense."(11)

As an opening act, the rookie also learns to develop entire comedy routines. One technique for developing a routine is for the comic to analyze his material and bring together jokes that are related, e.g., jokes on family, jokes on sports, or jokes on a garage sale. John Roarke describes another approach for creating a comedy routine:

> If you're doing a joke, you're doing a concept. So, you say to yourself, "This is the concept I am developing. Have I gotten the most out of it? Can I go one step further with it?" Jokes are little scenes that can be strung together. You're doing one or two scenes from a whole story, and there's almost always another scene from the story that you can play out.
>
> That's why comics have "hunks." A hunk is four minutes of fifteen jokes that hang together. When you write, you are often writing off of the stuff you already have. So, when you write a joke, ask yourself if you have milked

> every possible piece of humor out of that concept.[27]

To impress audiences, the novice also learns to devote some time to developing a chunk of "killer" material. Comedian/actor Richard Belzer, for example, notes that developing at least one minute of extremely funny material is one way to make sure that audiences (and club owners) will remember the performer as having been funny (Belzer, 1988).

As an opener, the young comic also learns editing skills that will help to improve his act. Comic John Wing illustrates:

> You get your first fifteen to twenty minutes of material. You start working as an opening act. But, before you middle, you will probably get rid of most of it and write a new thirty minutes that has more style and more polish. You have to cut down and throw stuff away. You get rid of the clutter. You get rid of the stuff that "ain't" jokes. You get rid of the stuff that is too long, and you get rid of the stuff that works, but isn't you.[28]

Kevin Jordan agrees, and provides the following example:

> I kept telling one young comic who does this joke where he grabs his crotch, "You don't need that. Drop that joke." He said, "But it's funny. It's killing." And, I said, "You...don't... need...it."

> I think back to a bit I used to have. I used to use a toilet seat as a pair of lips. It was hilarious; it rocked the roof. But, even my wife told me, "That joke is horrible." I said, "What are you talking about? They love that joke." But, she was right. It was really an offensive joke, and I should have dropped it a long time before I did.[54]

Trying out New Material

As an opening act, the novice learns when and where to try out his new material. For example, the rookie may learn to cushion his new material by placing it in the middle of his act or by placing it in between two jokes that usually get a laugh. Comic Ron Richards explains:

> I make joke Oreos. I do the new stuff in between two delicious pieces of tried and true material. You want to do some good pieces first. That way, you know that you are working well and that your material is working normally. Then you try the new bit, so that if it doesn't work well, you can recover with your proven material.[25]

The young comic also learns to try out his new material with a smaller crowd. Ron Richards explains the logic behind this strategy:

> The other way to try out new material is to come to a place where there's only 30 or 40 people. If there are 300

> people in a room and you don't get a laugh, that's a *big* empty space. If there are 30 people and the joke doesn't get a laugh, it doesn't sound so bad.[25]

<u>Learning to Manage Dry Spells and Plateaus</u>

As the young comic masters the process of building his minutes, he must also learn how to handle "growing pains," how to weather "dry" periods, and how to negotiate growth spurts. Comic John Caponera, for example, recalls his growing pains this way:

> For the longest time I just did this ten-minute bit because I knew it worked. When I began working on the road, I gradually started breaking in other material. I would talk about what I did and what was happening to me on the road. The more comfortable you get on stage, the more you start to take chances with new stuff.
>
> Also, you reach a point where you start going, "Man, I have to start working the crowd; my act is getting stale." You are almost forced to write new stuff.[13]

Comic Tim Jones recalls encountering his first "dry spell" as a writer this way:

> I got really paranoid about my first dry spell. This was open or middle time. I

> saw Rodney Dangerfield on a talk show, and he said that he had dry spells, too, and that everybody goes through it, and that it's okay. Man, I was listening to him like he was talking to me personally. Then, I said to myself, "It's okay, kid, it's 'gonna' rain."[(12)]

Finally, Paul Dillery describes the plateaus and growth spurts he experienced this way:

> For the longest time, I had only twelve minutes. I couldn't seem to get past it. Then, all of a sudden, bang, I had twenty minutes. It came in five-minute chunks somehow. Then, I was stuck at twenty-five minutes for the longest time. Then, I jumped to thirty-five or forty minutes. Then, I realized that I could middle, because I had more than a half-hour of material to choose from.[(24)]

Although his material may not yet "say" anything profound, the young comic starts to develop material that gives him confidence in his writing ability—and a sense of professionalism. Comic John Wing explains:

> After about two years, I wrote an important joke. It was important because it made me realize that I was very funny. That joke made me laugh out loud when I thought of it, and I realized that I could write funny things.

> It was a clean joke. It was well put together, and it was just a joke that gave me a lot of confidence.[28]

Finally, one comedian sums up the progress the young comic makes with writing during the opening act phase as follows:

> By the time you move into middle, you have the confidence that they *will* laugh, you have a better idea of *why* they'll laugh, and you are getting to know *when* they will laugh.[28]

<u>Learning about Timing, Delivery, and Other Performance Techniques</u>

At the same time the rookie is learning how to write, he is also learning how to perform. One element of performance technique is timing. Comic John Caponera speaks for several comics when he asserts that, "You can't teach timing." Caponera explains:

> [Comedic timing] is an inborn thing. Unless the performer has a natural kind of timing, there's no way they're ever going to get it. And if they do, it won't be natural. It'll feel synthetic, and the audience will sense it. They won't know what they're sensing, but the audience will know something is not right.[13]

Although timing and a "feel" for comedy may be instinctive, there are some aspects of stand-up technique that can be learned (e.g., stepping forward slightly on the punch line). Several comics indicate that they learned the technical aspects of the craft by watching other comics. One comic describes the process of learning to perform as follows:

> You start talking with other comics and you see technical things, like when to drop a certain word, when to pause, and when to make a "look," do a double take, use physical shtick, use a funny word, or use a funny inflection.(30)

Other comics indicate that a major component of learning delivery involves experimentation. Paul Dillery illustrates:

> Each time you get up there, you learn what is going to work with the crowd; for example, what pace (fast or slow), and what kind of material (clever, dirty, or high energy).
>
> Also, you'll work with a joke a while and say, "Well, tonight, I'm just going to throw it away and do it deadpan." If you get a big laugh, you go, "Wow, so that's how to do it. I was trying too hard with it."
>
> Then, too, you'll find that certain things work if you make a certain move, and you remember that. You'll go, "Hey, that works funny if I bend my knees at that point," and then you'll try it again.(24)

Mastering the delivery of a joke also involves learning the painstaking process of "crafting a joke." Crafting a joke means that the comic goes on stage each night for weeks or months and works with a joke little by little, changing a reference, saying the punch line a little louder, or doing the set up a little differently in an effort to determine the optimal delivery. Comedian John Caponera explains:

> You deliver a line you know is funny, but it doesn't get the laughs you know it should be getting. So, you might omit a couple of words or deliver it a different way, and all of a sudden it hits, and you say, "Wow, all I've got to do is switch it around and deliver it like this!"
>
> Every comic knows when they've got it though. They know when they hit it right. So much of this business is trial and error. It's just being able to stay with it and play with it and, eventually, if you are funny, it will come out. It's just being able to persevere, stay with your own sense of funny, and keep your confidence. Then, if it doesn't work out after so many times, you chuck it.(13)

Another element of perfecting delivery involves *consistency* in performing a joke. Once he discovers the most effective way to perform a joke, the comic must still learn how to deliver his material in a consistent manner *each time he performs it*. John Wing estimates that it can take up to a year to write three good jokes, link them together, and learn to perform them properly. He adds, "Sometimes you have to do it 40 or 50 times."[28]

In addition to becoming consistent, the young comedian also learns how to *persevere on stage* and how to *win over an audience*. Comedian Ron Richards illustrates:

> As an opening act, you learn *how not to give up*, and you learn how to *just keep going*. You learn that bombing is the most important part of learning the craft. That's where you learn your finesse. The difference between the guy who is a pro and the novice is that the pro just keeps working; he doesn't lose his cool. The guy who's an amateur falls apart.
>
> When I first started, I saw Glen Hirsch go up one night and he did not get many laughs. Only he didn't mention it. He just kept talking as if those things were just his conversation. He kept doing his act. He did about fifty minutes and eventually got a standing ovation from those people. I was impressed by that. I realized that if you don't let the audience know things are very bad, and that they (the audience) stink, you'll be okay. You can turn it around.[25]

Comedian Kip Adotta performs a "bit" that neatly summarizes some other things the comic learns about delivery. In this bit, Adotta teaches the audience to repeat along with him, "You *commit* to the joke, you go *straight through* the joke, and you don't *ask permission* to do the joke."

Adotta's routine illustrates several important concepts. First, the comic should go on stage with an attitude that says, "I am a funny person. This is funny material. I know it, and I expect you to get it." Next, the comic must deliver the material smoothly and without hesitation. Finally, the comic should covey an attitude of being in control. He has the microphone, and it is his *job* to entertain. As one comic described it, "When you have the microphone, you own the room. Nobody should be louder than you. You're like a lion tamer with a whip: you're in control."(5)

<u>Learning to Interact Effectively with Audiences</u>

For most comics, part of acquiring a professional demeanor includes learning how to interact effectively with audiences. Many comics learn to interact with audiences by asking audience members, "Where are you from?" and "What do you do?" Paul Dillery states that he would sometimes prompt the audience by saying, "Any questions?" when he wanted to be asked things for which he wasn't prepared. This technique helped him learn to work off the top of his head.(24)

Dillery describes another strategy that he used when he first started interacting with audiences. He recalls:

> You make notes about the questions audience members ask, and then you go home and make up jokes about what they asked. So, the next time they ask the same question you are prepared for it, and they go, "Oh,

> he's a genius. He made that up on the spot."[24]

Comics also prepare "spontaneous" ad libs for those times when they ask an audience member where he or she is from or what he or she does for a living. Over time, the comic thus accumulates pre-planned responses for many occupations and locations that are guaranteed to get a laugh *and* appear spontaneous.

Like developing a comic persona and learning to write, a comic improves his audience skills based on the amount of stage time he gets as an opening act. Good audience skills can take several years to develop.

Learning the Role of Master of Ceremonies

In addition to acquiring audience interaction skills and learning to perform a solid fifteen-minute set, the rookie comic also learns how to serve as Master of Ceremonies during the opening act phase. The Master of Ceremonies (MC) introduces each act, and confers with each of the performers to be sure that he mentions the performer's television or film credits, awards, and upcoming appearances correctly. Comic Kevin Jordan describes his approach to MC'ing this way:

> My attitude was, when you MC, don't do any material. Your job is just to set up the show. The Opener, Middle, and the Headliner are coming up behind you, and *they* are doing the show. Your job as MC is to keep that show flowing. To do that, you just talk to the audience. You find out if

> there are any birthdays or if someone is getting married, etc. Of course, everybody has his own style. The main thing is that the MC plays a key role because he has to hold the whole show together.[54]

John Wing describes some of the other skills required of an MC:

> It's the MC's responsibility to make sure that the show is very good. He must make the other guys look good and also has to be very funny himself. The host teaches the audience how to listen. The host should relax the group. He must get them used to somebody talking to them, and make sure they heckle him and not the other comics on the show.[28]

Comedian Steve McGrew observes, "Unfortunately, some guys have a hard time with MC'ing." McGrew explains:

> Some comics think MC'ing is below them. A lot of guys say, "My act goes better if I'm not the MC." Or, there are guys who say, "I just have to come out and hit them with my material." But, I say, "MCing is an important skill, and you very well may be MC'ing or opening for a star someday."[44]

Rocky LaPorte agrees that learning to MC is a critical skill for the young comic to develop. LaPorte recalls, "One of the best things anyone ever did for me was to keep me MCing in order for me to build that skill."

Comedian Kevin Jordan, for example, reports that working as an MC helped him with his "*audience skills*." He states that, "As an MC, it became second nature for me to talk with someone whom I hadn't met before." Dan Smith indicates that he learned "*really good crowd control*" from hosting a rowdy room. Smith explains:

> I learned how to deal with drunk people, people who wanted to be the center of attention, and people whose intent it was to disrupt the show.[61]

Finally, Rocky LaPorte sums up the importance of learning to MC this way:

> Building your MC skills is like constructing a building. If you have a good foundation—if you are a good MC—then you can do anything. Really good comics are asked to host the Emmys and the Oscars—and they do it. Moreover, they are *good* at hosting *because* they had built a solid foundation.[42]

Learning to Handle Hecklers and Other Interruptions

As an opening act, the young comic must learn how to deal with both subtle and rowdy interruptions of his delivery. The rookie quickly discovers that the delivery of a line is a very fragile thing, and that even a very good joke can be ruined easily. For instance, if someone speaks too loudly or puts a drink down too loudly just as the comic delivers the joke, the noise may drown out the set up or punch line, and/or draw the focus from the comic. Similarly, if someone gets up to go to the restroom in a disruptive manner, everyone will look over and the effect of the comic's set up or punch line can be ruined.

The novice comic soon learns that he must address such interruptions. As one comic describes it, "When something happens, if everybody saw or heard it, you can't just ignore it, so, you try to make it funny." Thus, at the opening act stage the comic learns techniques for *making* interruptions funny. For example, he learns to add comments like the following to his repertoire:

- What is this, tag team bathroom? Anybody else "got to go" while I'm on stage?

- Just set that glass down anywhere, why don't you?

As he gains experience, the comic will learn other ways to acknowledge an incident and make an interruption funny. For example, one evening a patron dropped a drink at his table. A club staff member dutifully marched down the aisle toward the stage with a broom and a dustpan to clean the broken glass. However, this food server was oblivious to the fact that his actions had drawn the focus from the comic and brought the show to a momentary standstill. Without missing a beat, the headliner on stage, Michael Loftus, started to improvise. He began to silently mimic the staff member's clean-up efforts. By staying cool and by being creative, the veteran comic regained the audience's focus and created a very funny, spontaneous moment out of the interruption. This is exactly the kind of skill that a young comic might make note of, lend his unique comic touch to, and then add to his bag of tricks.

At this stage, the comic also learns how to deal with rowdier interruptions of his act such as heckling. The novice comic typically learns to respond instantly and decisively to a heckler, and he begins to add heckler retorts to his act. A young comic might learn heckler put downs such as the following:

- Why don't you two team up and form a moron?
- I guess we forgot to put up the "12-IQ minimum" sign tonight.
- How old were you when your mind first got up and walked away from you?

As comic Larry Omaha recalls, "Heckling bothered me so much that I vowed I was never going to let a heckler get the last word again." Omaha adds:

> I went home and spent two days focused on writing twenty heckler put-downs. I then memorized five of them immediately. I was determined to be ready the next time.(61)

Early on, the idea is for the young comic to "nip the heckling in the bud" with a heckler retort that's a sure-fire silencer. This practice also serves the function of suppressing "audience rebellion" before it spreads. Comic Rudy Moreno explains:

> At first you don't know what to do with hecklers. You get angry. It throws

> you off. Over the years, you learn how to handle hecklers. *You use a heckler put-down and get back into your act.* But, you always have to top a heckler, because if you can't, you're done. The rest of the audience will jump in.[43]

In addition to heckler putdowns, the young comic also learns techniques for re-establishing control. One subtle technique cited by the comics is to walk up in front of a couple who are chattering and raise one's voice level. The comic's presence, along with the raised voice, generally will get their attention. A second technique a comic may use to regain control is to initiate interaction with the person in the audience who looks most bored (a.k.a., "the comedy challenge"). Talking to this audience member frequently serves to defuse a potential heckler.

In order to avoid alienating the rest of the audience when he responds to a heckler, the rookie also learns techniques such as how to repeat the heckler's remark so that the whole audience hears it. The following quote by John Caponera illustrates the value of this simple action:

> Somebody said something in the front row, and I blew up at them. The whole audience got mad at me because I didn't repeat what the guy had said over the microphone. The back of the room didn't realize what he'd been saying to me, and they thought I was just jumping on the guy. So, when anybody yells out something, I always repeat it into the mic so the whole room will know what has happened.[13]

As an opening act, the comic learns how to survive the worst audiences and the worst clubs. Several comics recommend that under impossible circumstances, the novice should do his set and consider the time as a vocal exercise or use it to work on movement, improvising, or something else. If the audience is drunk or small, the comic should view the set as an opportunity to learn how to deal with those situations. As one comic observes:

> Somehow you've got to galvanize your hide. That happens by getting up on stage and failing a lot. But that is the forge in which the metal is tempered. When you go through so much of that, and when you can withstand the worst, then when you get into the better situations, you are cool under fire. You get to the point where almost nothing ruffles you.[2]

With practice, the comic's material, delivery, and audience management skills all fall into place, and the *major components of stand-up comedy start to work together the way they are intended.* Several comics report that this important plateau often occurs one night while the comic is on stage.[21, 31]

It is also a very exciting moment for the comic when one's material and delivery come together and a new joke works on stage. One comic describes this moment as follows:

> My favorite thing in the whole world is when my new bits work on stage. It's like, "Aww, my new kid." It really is like your kid, you know. It's a great feeling!

Interestingly, the comics report that the processes of developing a comic persona, learning to write, and mastering performance skills are strongly interrelated. For example, the better the comic knows himself, the more he can focus his material when he writes. In addition, improved writing and performing also yield other benefits, as the following comedienne illustrates:

> As your delivery gets better, then you can use material that might have seemed more obscure to you when you were starting out. As you get more confidence in your ability to put it over, you try it. Sometimes, they get the weirder ones you thought that they wouldn't get.(11)

The more skills the comics accumulated, the more confident they became. As they became more confident, they began having more good sets—and fewer really bad performances.

<u>Noticing More about One's Surroundings and Learning about Different Venues</u>

When the comic first starts performing, his focus is inward, i.e., on his fear and self-consciousness. As John Caponera describes it:

> When you first go up, you are so wrapped up and worried about bombing and delivering your stuff right, and getting off safe—literally surviving—that you're oblivious to everything else.(13)

However, once the comic becomes more relaxed on stage, he is then free to focus on his external surroundings. It is at this point that he begins to notice things about the rooms in which he performs. One comedienne, for example, indicates that she started to notice "pictures on the walls and objects in the room that she had not noticed before."[(11)] By the end of this stage, the young comic starts *looking for* funny things about the room that can help him tailor his performance.

Several comics also report that at this stage they began to notice the subtle qualities of the different rooms in which they performed. For example, they notice that they must get used to playing each new room. They also discover that they like playing certain rooms rather than others because of the "good feeling" a room has.

The comics also begin to learn about performing in venues of different sizes. For example, they find that small rooms can be very intimate. As one comic describes it, "In a small room, it's looser. You can have fun with the audience. You can make funny asides, and even do stuff for the other comics." Small crowds also tend to require a lot of one-on-one interaction. John Caponera explains:

> I used to think, "Oh my God, there are only ten people. What am I going to do?" Then, I'd go on stage and make mention of it, have fun with it, and right away they'd loosen up.
>
> What you do with a small crowd is to talk to them. You find out where they are from, and what they do, and then you work off of that. You see if *they*

> can give *you* anything funny. Then, you can get into your act; but you have to walk out easy and develop some rapport first.[13]

As Ron Richards reports, with a small group the young comic learns to make his material conversational:

> In a small club, the big laughs aren't there, and there isn't a lot of time in between the jokes. A lot of times, you can stand up there and think, "Well, what am I going to do next?" while they are laughing. With a small crowd you can't do that, so you just keep it moving.
>
> I put in a lot of extra thoughts, as well as new material, and I make it more like it is just a conversation. That way, if a joke doesn't get a laugh it's like, "I was just talking."[25]

In large venues, the comic must play things a little broader in the theatrical sense, as Eddie Merrill explains:

> If you're performing for a concert-sized crowd, everything you do has to be bigger so that people in the back seats can see you. You have to be a little bit bigger in your physical actions and what you have to say.[21]

Comic Rocky LaPorte agrees and adds, "On larger stages you need to be a little more animated. You might have to move around a little more. And in theaters, you must work slower because the room is bigger and it takes longer for the laughter to roll through."

Learning about the Properties of Energy in a Room

Some comics indicate that as an opening act they started becoming aware of a property they called "energy." It was a rudimentary awareness at this point. They were not yet able to "read" a room well or "shift the energy of a room" with any consistency. However, an awareness of at least two kinds of energy was present at this stage. The comics spoke of becoming aware of the energy that they were giving off, and the energy that was coming from the audience. Tim Jones, for example, describes the energy he was generating this way:

> I was always so full of energy. I'd get up on stage, and I'd go full force. I used to take off like a rocket. I'd blow the people in the front row away. It took me a while to learn how to control myself. Then, I had to learn how to combine the two. I had to be energetic when that was called for, and be more relaxed when that was appropriate.(12)

Several comics also report that at this stage they were beginning to become aware of the energy that emanated from audiences. They describe being able to "feel the audience slip away," and they were also aware when they had done something that had "captured the audience's attention."

As an opening act, the comic learns to watch movement around the room, and he starts to listen to the audience's reactions. In this way, the comic gradually learns how to "read" the audience's energy level, and he learns how to "play off of" the audience's responses. However, as one comic remarks, "sometimes they fool you." Nick Gaza explains:

> Usually, if the audience laughs at a joke it's your cue to go ahead with another joke along similar lines. But, sometimes, they'll tighten up at the second joke you do, and you just go, "Huh? You laughed the first time."

By the three-year mark, the comic is also becoming more aware of various elements that can influence energy in a room. For example, the comics state that the news of the day and the particular day of the week affect an audience's energy level. They report, for instance, that a local or national tragedy will bring a crowd's energy level down. Conversely, a holiday weekend generally means the crowd will be in a good mood. A playoff loss by a local sports team or the death a beloved national figure can also negatively affect the audience's mood and, thus, represent a challenge for the comic.

As an opener, the young comic also learns about different types of individual audience members. In addition to "the drunk" the comic also encounters audience members such as the "mean one," "the talker" and "the person who wants attention, badly."

"Laugh Leaders" are an element of the audience that can positively or negatively influence the crowd. One comic states that, "It is almost as though some audience members become row leaders or leaders for their section."(2) One comedienne describes her experience with positive laugh leaders this way:

> I like laugh leaders. Usually they're all men or all women. They are there to have a good time, and they are not intimidated by being with a date. If there is a group of laugh leaders, then all it takes is a group like that, and the whole audience begins laughing.[11]

An example of the negative energy laugh leaders can exert is the case of "bad vibes" emanating from an individual or a small group. For instance, comedienne Diane Nichols states that, "You can always tell the couple that just had a fight or the couple that was outvoted and didn't want to be there."

Some comics develop a greater awareness of "energy" than others, and some comics learn to manipulate the energy and use it to better advantage than others. While the comic's sensitivity to the energy in a room begins as an opener, it is generally more fully developed as a middle act.

Learning about Diverse Audiences

During the second and third years of performing, the comic starts to work with diverse audiences. The young comic soon comes to think of audiences as more than just a collection of individuals. He learns that each audience seems to take on its own personality. As one comic describes it, "Each audience is its own animal." With experience, the comic learns to distinguish each audience's personality.

Comics come to identify many different types of audiences. For example, there are small audiences/large audiences;

hip audiences/slow audiences; urban audiences/rural audiences; yuppie audiences/redneck audiences; liberal audiences/conservative audiences; older audiences/younger audiences; easy audiences and difficult audiences. One comic describes "cerebral audiences with whom you can get clever,"[5] and "drunk audiences who will only respond to vulgar language and crotch humor."[2] Ultimately, the young comic learns that analyzing the audience either before he goes up or shortly thereafter, can help him to tailor his performance.

Learning about Audience Expectations

In addition to learning to perform for different types of audiences, the comic also learns about "audience expectations." For example, the comics report that audiences like it when the comic is personal: they like getting to know something about the comic.

Rookies also learn that audiences like to see honesty and they like to see things that are genuine. As one comic put it, "They don't want your problems, and they don't want to be bummed out; but they want you to be real."

Audiences also like fairness. Comic Steven Allen Green describes the audience's expectation of fairness this way:

> Audiences don't like the comic treating an audience member unjustly. If the comic reacts too harshly to someone who was just joining in rather than heckling, the audience won't back you up. They'll go, "Hey, he was just trying to help out."[18]

Comic Jimmy Burns observes that, "The audience will tolerate a lot and they will give you a lot of freedom if you show them respect." He adds, "Part of that respect is always being professional and expressing your appreciation for the time they have allowed you to share with them."[39] Therefore, most comics will close their set with some variation of "Thank you. You guys have been great," or, "Good night. You guys have been a lot of fun." Moreover, even when the set has *not* gone well, a comic may acknowledge the audience with, "Thank you. You've been a patient audience."

<u>"Good" Audiences</u>

In addition to learning about audience expectations, the young comic also learns the qualities that make for "good" audiences. One comic, for example, describes good audiences as being attentive: they *want* to be entertained, and they will sit there, quietly, and let themselves be entertained."[39] Good audiences are also good-natured, and they are loose enough to laugh.[18, 5]

Good audiences are also paying audiences. As one comic put it, "The more they pay, the more attentive and well-behaved audiences are. When the cover charge is low or admission is free, the crowd tends to heckle more freely."[5] When they pay to see a show, audiences want to make certain that they have a good time and most audience members tend to be on their best behavior.

Several comics also assert that a good audience can be both a friend and valued ally. For example, one comic states, "If you endear yourself to them, the audience will take care of hecklers for you."[5] In addition, a good audience can have a "Wow, you're really great—we're having fun—please don't leave" attitude that is wonderful for the comic's ego.[4]

The young comic further discovers that there is a reciprocal relationship with the audience. The comic gives the audience something (laughter, a release, and self-recognition), and the audience gives something to the comic (approval, affection, and his livelihood). In addition, if they are attentive, audiences can provide excellent feedback for the comic's new material. As one comic describes it:

> Sometimes when you do something new, they'll go "Oooooh" instead of laugh. A lot of times that "Oooooh" is better than a laugh because you know that they were paying attention, and you go, "Good! Maybe it's a little too dirty. I can re-adjust a few words, and it'll get a laugh the next time."[5]

"Bad" Audiences

As an opening act, the rookie also begins to form his definition of "bad" audiences. Comic Jim Shubert offers the following example:

> I'm from the school that didn't think there are bad crowds. But, yeah, there really are bad crowds. It can be from the guy who went on before you who changed the mood of the room, to the fact that the crowd is already drunk and rowdy at the late show, and they are just screaming, "Woo, woo."[3]

Most frequently, bad audiences are described by comics as drunken audiences. Drunken audiences may yell things out randomly or even throw things at the performer during his show. Drunken audiences also don't want to think; they only want the "easy" (i.e., dirty) material, and this can be frustrating for a comic who enjoys doing topical, clever, or thought-provoking material.

Some bad audiences are "low energy" audiences. There are nights when almost nobody over the course of an evening can inject much life into an audience. Sometimes, bad audiences won't stop chattering. In such instances, the comic may try kidding the crowd about the incessant talking. He may try appealing to them, or he may insult the offending audience member(s). When all else fails, the comic may signal the management to remove a particularly disruptive patron.

Bad audiences also can be unsatisfying for the comic for other reasons, as the following comic illustrates:

> Sometimes, I go up and it is an ugly audience. There's something ugly in the air. I'll do well, but they'll laugh at the wrong things, and I won't feel comfortable with them. I won't give them my all, because they don't deserve me. Some audiences I want to give everything to.[(28)]

When he encounters a bad audience, the young comic must learn to deal with the cards he has been dealt. As one comic put it, "You do the best with what you've got."[(5)] If his material is not working, sometimes the comic may turn to the old "talk-to-the-audience" trick.[(24)] Another comic notes, "Sometimes, working the audience can be funnier than the material you were going to do for that group."[39] Comic Jim Shubert adds:

> Getting them to be quiet and pay attention, that all comes in the craft. That's all in the honing. You learn how to control that. You learn how to play a moment, take it, turn it around, and make it yours. You learn how to take control of a room.[3]

Finding *Your* Audience

Toward the mid-point of the opening act stage, the rookie also starts to find his target audience. As one young comic describes it:

> I finally had a gig that introduced me to *my* audience. They didn't have to get to know me, and I didn't have to warm up to them. I knew then exactly who my target audience was. I knew what direction to take my comedy.[23]

Discovering one's audience may also occur later in one's career, as Tom Ryan explains:

> I was a low-key act, and I had trouble on the road. The late night crowds weren't listening. They wouldn't "get" me. For a long time, club owners did not see me as a powerful enough act to close all seven shows for the week. Then, I found that I was much better as a concert opener, and I found my crowd at corporate gigs.[64]

"Studying" the Audience

To tailor his act and succeed with different audiences, the young comic learns to study an audience by watching the previous performer(s). One reason for observing the audience is so the comic can determine what material he can and cannot do. By "casing" the showroom, the comic can also get a sense of what topics peak the audience's interest.

In addition to allowing the comic to pick up an audience's vibe, watching the previous performer(s) also helps the comic to know what material has already been covered. A brief mention of another performer's material can establish continuity in a show and provide the appearance of spontaneity even when it to leads to an established bit by the comic.

Some comedians report that they like to peek out at a crowd from behind the stage curtain to get a better sense of the audience's composition and energy. Surveying the crowd provides the comic with such information as, "How many gray-haired audience members are there?" and "Are they all seventeen-year-old 'punkers' waiting for a rock band?" This information helps the comic to select appropriate material for that group.[13, 28]

One comedienne reports that she assesses the audience when she goes to the ladies room:

> I didn't realize I was doing this, but I go to the ladies room and I usually put on my make-up again because it's often faded by the time I arrive at the club. Women come in there, and you can hear their conversations. You just get a sense of what they are like.[11]

"Is the Audience with Me?"

The young comic learns that an audience must be monitored. Audiences can be warm and cooperative, but they are also a fickle entity. According to several comics, you can lose the audience in just a few seconds, particularly if you anger them.[39] Hence, the struggle to win and hold the audience can be a constant battle while the comic is on stage. One comic describes the process of monitoring audiences this way:

> What goes through my mind is, "Do they like me? Are they with me?" Then, after a while (it could be one minute or five minutes), I go, "All right, they like me. Are they still with me?" It's a constant struggle. Sometimes it's not a big struggle, but it is something you always have in mind on stage.

Comic John Roarke describes his experience with monitoring audiences this way:

> You feel if they like you and if they are following you by their response. It's like a relationship between any two people. You can even explain their characteristics to another comic: "They were a little more this way or that way." But you always *feel* where they are by their response.[27]

Re-gaining Control of the Audience (a.k.a., "Cracking the Comedy Whip")

If the comic starts to lose an audience, audience members may begin to talk, they may heckle, or they may greet him with dead silence. The comic must then take action to re-gain control. He may try his best material. He may try to silence the pockets of talking by teasing the individual or group, or he may kid the audience about its lack of response. Some types of good-natured kidding by the comic include the following comments:

- It's like pulling teeth up here! You guys are really putting me through hell, aren't you?
- You really know how to hurt a guy, don't you?
- You know, if you guys get the jokes, we'll all get out of here a lot sooner!
- Is this an oil painting or an audience?

A comic's initial heckler put-down will usually suffice to silence a heckler and permit the comic to regain control. However, even when he is heckled, the young comic is continuing to learn. He is learning how to *stay calm after the initial heckle*, and he is *learning to respond to the heckler* with additional heckler put-downs that may be more direct or more insulting.

As an opening act, the comic is also learning how to *weather a comeback by the heckler.* As comic John Wing points out, "Eventually the comic learns that even if the audience laughs at what the heckler says, it's okay. Their laughter gives *him* more time to think of something that's even funnier."[28]

At this stage, the comic learns to rely on the quick-wittedness that he has been developing to pull difficult situations out of the fire. Moreover, the comic is accumulating a larger and more sophisticated repertoire of potential remedies that will allow him to assess the damage and regain control.

The more experience he has with audiences and the larger his bag of tricks, the more confidence the comic develops in his ability to handle diverse audiences and bad situations. Moreover, as the young comic reviews the way he handled a tough situation on stage, the comic's sense of professionalism is reinforced.

Learning to Make a Living at Comedy

By the two-year mark, the comic is generally seasoned enough to work as an opening act. He may also be a paid regular at a showcase club. In each case, the young comic now has access to regular stage time. When he begins to get work as an opening act, he may give up a day job to commit full-time to comedy. Because he cannot support himself by getting on stage for one or two spots per week at a showcase club, the young comic is also struggling to earn a living. He must learn how to get other bookings.

Several comics report that they got performing spots by contacting a club owner who basically said, "Okay, kid, show me what you can do." Other comics indicate that they found out about a club booker or a new place to contact by "talking to other comics" and "keeping their ears to the tracks."

The comics also recall supporting themselves at this stage by playing at Moose Lodges, Elks Clubs, church functions, supermarket openings, talent nights, bingo halls, and community festivals. As one comic put it, "At a later stage in your career, you would never do some of these gigs again; but, in the beginning, they provide both the seasoning and the income the comic needs."[(39)]

Interestingly, the comics report that the ethnic communities to which they belong provide an important source of work for them. For example, African American, Latino, and Asian comics report tapping into a wide array of community organizations and activities. One African American comedienne, Robin Cee, indicates that she had started performing for her church at various functions and built a reputation that way. As a result of this exposure, she regularly got other work in the black community. Other ethnic comics report a similar experience in their communities.

However, while ethnic communities may be supportive early on, they may also be limiting for the young comic in ways that he may not anticipate. Comedian Rudy Moreno explains:

> In the last ten years, a lot of Latino comic nights have popped up. You'll get a young guy who is starting out, and he will think everything he said is funny because that particular group can relate to it. But then, they get a gig in Iowa, and the same material is going over the crowd's head and he doesn't understand why.
>
> It is important for young, ethnic comics to understand that they are going to be working for all kinds of crowds. If you are going to be a headliner across this country, you are going to have to be able to perform for all types of audiences. The ethnic comic must broaden his or her horizons, and develop more universal topics with general appeal.[4]

Starting to Have Fun with Stand-Up

The comedian exposes a great deal of himself through his stand-up and, as noted earlier, audience rejection can be devastating. However, by the end of the opening act phase, the comic has developed his skills to the point where he also starts to enjoy the some of the rewards of his profession.

When asked, "What are the best things about doing stand-up?" the comics invariably reply, "the attention" or "the recognition." Comic Jeff Cesario explains:

> It sounds selfish, but the attention is just great. Sometimes you just stop, especially when the crowd is with you and you're really rolling, and you have that extra second or two to breathe, and you just let them laugh, and you think, "They're laughing at s--t I made up!" Through all the writing process you hope for it, but when you actually see it, you think, "They're laughing at s--t I made up—and they want more!" What a great way to make a living![32]

Several comics report that they love being in the position of having a forum on stage that few others have. Other comics enjoy having the opportunity to be heard. Jeff Cesario provides the following example:

> The best thing about stand-up comedy is that I get to say the things I really feel. I don't think there's any huge

> message in what I'm doing; a lot of my stuff is just for "yuks." But, there are important things you can do with your comedy, and that's a blast. The more leverage I get in the business, the more I hope I can incorporate more of that kind of stuff in my act.[32]

Many comics indicate that they love doing stand-up because it is a natural mood-elevator for them. They state that they often cracked themselves up with the things they thought on stage. They, too, enjoy it when there is a snappy, good-natured back-and-forth with the audience.[39] The comics explain that laughter is infectious, and that they frequently wind up having a good time on stage, even when the evening hadn't started that way. Several comics even state that a good set can relieve a headache or minor cold symptoms.[33, 25]

The comics also cite *unity with audiences* and *a feeling of power* as two additional rewards from performing stand-up comedy. Comedian/actor Jeff Altman sums up the love one feels and the feeling of control that the comic derives from doing stand-up this way:

> For me, it is a sublimated form of love in the sense that you learn to reinforce yourself through the laughs alone. Some people's reinforcement for what they do is the money they make. But, you'll find that most comedians, if given a place where they can't earn money, will still go on stage and do jokes. There is no more instant gratification than laughter. Even a

> hug sometimes isn't as great as having 200 or 300 people in a room bending over with laughter. I mean, it's a form of power. It's a form of control. It really satisfies a lot of the basic needs of man.[14]

Jeff Altman further observes that although stand-up is a craft and a skill one develops, "it might be tied in a little more to the immediate existence of a comic." Altman states:

> A comedian becomes intimately tied to what he is doing in terms of his power. If it's a guy, sometimes his masculinity and his own sense of success are tied into the telling of jokes.[14]

Several comics also describe the satisfaction they derive from doing stand-up in terms of "audience seduction." As one comic put it, "From time-to-time, when everything comes together just right, a little magic is created for both the performer and the audience." On those nights, the comic is exciting the audience and the audience is feeding positive energy and love back to the comic. The energy that results is not unlike a climax between two lovers. For the audience, there is side-splitting laughter; and, for the comic:

> It is the climax between power and the need for love; and, when that happens, it is an explosion.[14]

The excerpts above suggest that for many comedians, audiences are an important source of emotional sustenance.

Several comics even use the analogy of an "addiction" to describe the feeling they get from performing. As one comic described it, "Just about the time I get discouraged about the business, I'll perform for a hot crowd, get an enormous rush, and I'll get 'hooked' again."[39]

Born of a Humanitarian Spirit

The comics also state that they derive great satisfaction from being involved in an enterprise that makes other people happy. They take great pride in the fact that they can make people forget their troubles for a while. Jeff Cesario expresses the satisfaction he gets from performing this way:

> I get a kick from people walking up to me and saying, "You were funny; I really enjoyed your show." All of a sudden I feel, "Well, I've not only gotten my attention, but I've added something to someone's day that they didn't have before they walked in." I think that is very important.[32]

Dan Smith agrees and adds that:

> If you can make them laugh and forget about their day, their lives, or whatever is on their mind, it's an overwhelming feeling of success. I'm sure the rush is different for every comic; but, the rush I get is *they are forgetting about everything else except laughing at what I just said.*[61]

Barbara's "Take" on the Opening Act Phase

As an opening act, the comic reaches a basic level of competency with all of the major skills required by the craft. Writing and performing have begun to work together. The comic has begun to explore his comic style. He has started to use all of his senses—his eyes, his ears, his comedic instinct, his experiences on stage (good and bad), and his gut feelings—to help him handle all of things that can happen on stage.

In addition, the comic has begun the process of accumulating exposure to different audiences, different rooms, different sound systems, and different acoustics—all things that he will need in order to do the job. Finally, by the end of this career stage, the comic has started to acquire the thick hide and grace under pressure required by the art form.

Although the individual timetables for mastering the foregoing skills may vary, the opening act phase *is the period during which a solid foundation for performing stand-up comedy is laid.*

Becoming One with the Space

The more you do it, the more you get a picture of the canvas. As an opener, you don't fully know the space or what you can do with the space yet, but you're getting an idea of what the space is. And, the more you do it, the more you become a part of it.

Some Goals at the Two-Year Mark

- To get a taste of the road.
- To work on spontaneity and improv skills.
- To find the best way to express physicality, i.e., to improve mannerisms and movement.
- To improve utilization of the stage.
- To delve deeper into family and childhood experiences for material.
- To expand/get deeper into one's impressions.
- To further develop twenty solid minutes.
- To become a good audience warm-up.

Jeffrey Peterson

The Voice of Experience

You are ready for the next step when the act that follows you can't follow you - and that happens consistently.

If you want to headline in the "A" clubs, get up on stage as much as you can. Write, write, write. Put something on paper every day. Then, work the road. Use your time on the road to write. If this is your craft and this is truly something you want to do, then make it your job.

Record every set. Try a new joke every show. Develop a point of view that other people can identify.

You must have the material to obtain the headliner position, and you must have the performing power to sustain the position. Otherwise, you are not ready to headline in the "A" clubs. There are a lot of good people out there; therefore, you must take your job seriously.

Finally, when Richard Pryor got in trouble with a heckler, he went small. If you can't handle the heckler, go small: become humble and make yourself vulnerable. That way, you endear the audience to you and you turn them against the heckler. Once the audience is against the heckler, then YOU can turn against the heckler. It's a beautiful thing to watch the audience turn against the heckler.

Kivi Rogers

CHAPTER 5

THE MIDDLE ACT PHASE: YEARS 3 – 5
ADDING THE FINAL POLISH

LIFE ON THE ROAD

Hey, Anybody Here Know If You Can Make Ghosts Laugh?

One time we were at this hotel [out West]. It's an old hotel and it's reputed to have the spirits of people who died nearby. We comics would come in real late, and we started making ghost jokes. We joked that the ghosts got tired of waiting up for us. After joking around for a while and scaring ourselves, we started asking each other, "Can I sleep with you tonight?"

- Armando Cosio

Bilingual Faucets?

I went to take a shower at this same hotel, and there were two knobs for the shower and two knobs for the tub. But, all four knobs had the letter "C" on them. I got curious; so, I called down to room service and asked why all the knobs had a "C" on them. The guy from room service responded, "Oh, that's easy: one is for cold, the other is for *caliente* (Spanish for 'hot')." I'd forgotten that the city is bilingual!

- Armando Cosio

The "Downside" of Working the Road

People think this job is easy. It's not. You're traveling constantly. You can be crossing time zones, multiple times, within in a relatively short period. You fly into a city, do one or two shows that same night. You get into your hotel late. You're jet lagged. Then, you have to wake up early for a radio interview—and you're expected to be funny on demand. A lot of comics use sleeping pills or they use alcohol in order to sleep. At least when you are physically tired, you can rest; but, try being funny when you are emotionally tired. Now, multiply all of that times years of performing.

- Rocky LaPorte

Some Other Tough Aspects of Working the Road

Sometimes when you are on the road, all you see is the inside of the airport, the inside of the cab, the inside of your hotel room, and the inside of the club. You'll wake up and think, "What city am I in?" and you'll be surrounded by strangers a lot.

- Margaret Smith

Is This What You Call "Being Willing to Die for Your Art?"

The first several years there was a lot of sacrifice. In my first three years on the road, I made $7,000, $9,000, and $11,000. For three years I traveled all over the country. I couldn't stay in hotels. I had to sleep in my car. Often, I had to drive all night to the next job.

- Don Friesen

CHAPTER 5

THE MIDDLE ACT PHASE: YEARS 3 – 5
ADDING THE FINAL POLISH

Middle act is the "soft spot" in the line up. ... The audience is warmed up. They've eaten. They've already had their first drink; so, they are loose but not drunk. They're able to sit back and enjoy the show. ... You get to do more time (thirty minutes), but you don't have the pressure of closing the show.
Various comics

Overview of the Middle Act Phase

Once he has more than thirty minutes of consistent material, the comic may begin marketing himself as a middle act (also known as the "Feature Act"). As the quotation above suggests, the middle spot is considered the easy spot in the line up: the middle comic does not have the pressure of opening the show in front of a "cold" audience, and he does not have the responsibility of closing the show when audiences may be worn out. The middle act gets more time on stage to show his talent and practice his craft, yet he does not have the burden of performing for forty-five to sixty minutes, as does the headliner.

John Caponera recalls his experience at middle this way:

> Things came together for me as a middler. I grew the most when I middled because I took more chances. I knew that I could bomb and the show didn't depend on me.[13]

The middle act phase is a time for the comic to develop his persona, refine his material, and assemble a longer and more polished act. As a "middler," the comic is also learning to talk to the audience and "slide in and out of his material easily." In addition, before he headlines, the comic "must be able to field a ball coming at him from any direction, and he must be calm and confident about it."(15, 28) This career stage also introduces the comic to the business side of show business. The middle years add the final polish to the performer, and they prepare the comic to assume the responsibilities of headlining.

What Happens During the Middle Act Phase

The major skills and experiences of the feature act stage are:

- Finding one's comic persona
- Continued growth in writing, editing, and assembling an act
- Honing performing skills
- Developing versatility with audiences
- Learning about the business aspects of show business
- Getting television exposure
- Obtaining road experience

Finding One's Comic Persona

Most comics report that they found their comic persona or comic perspective as a middle act. In addition, many began searching for ways to get beyond making mundane observations during this stage. At middle, the comics also develop an image that is consistent with the way they look and sound.

It can take several years of performing to find out what is funny in yourself, to develop confidence in your "funny," and to bring your material to the point where you are willing to take the risk of revealing yourself to audiences. As one comic put it, the nature of stand-up is that you are essentially "putting yourself on the line."

Typically, the comic's stage persona contains one or more aspects of the comic's personality that "go across the footlights," (e.g., silliness or brashness). Often, the comic persona consists of various aspects of the comic's personality that become exaggerated for their humorous effect (e.g., cheapness or vanity).

Sometimes, the comic's viewpoint derives from his experiences (e.g., being a naïve youth from a rural area). Jim Shubert describes his on-stage persona as "turning on Personality Plus." Most comics fall in the category where they exaggerate their true characteristics.

The comic persona also can be a part of the comic's personality that he enjoys strengthening. For example, the comic may enjoy expanding the part of him that is in control. Comedienne Diane Nichols explains:

> It was fun for me to be in control on stage because in real life I didn't have a lot of control when I was young. I spent some time in the hospital, and I never got over feeling helpless.[4]

For other comedians, their comic viewpoint is something akin to an alter ego. One actress/comedienne indicates that her persona provides "a release from being nice." She states that she has expanded the part of her that doesn't edit herself and the part that lets her do what she wants. This comedienne further states that her persona has allowed her to say things she previously would never have thought of saying out loud.

Several comics indicate that the development of one's persona is intertwined with one's growth as a writer. As John Roarke explains, "The persona happens as you start to understand about writing your jokes. As you write better jokes, you zero in on what parts of yourself to magnify." Roarke also adds:

> What helped me most is the idea that the closer you are to *who you are exactly* and *what happens to you*, the better you become and the more honest your jokes are. Also, the more you stick to your own style, the less people can steal from you, and the less you can be accused of stealing from others.[27]

Comedian John Caponera states that refining his comic style involved trying out various tacks, and then combining those features with which he was most comfortable:

> At first I did impressions. Then I did one-liners. Then I did stories. I went through a lot of phases, and I did a lot of things trying to find my niche. Gradually, I realized that all of those things were a part of me. I'm not just a one-liner

> guy. I'm not strictly an impressionist. I'm not only a storyteller. It was all a part of me, and I discovered I could incorporate many of those things into my act.[13]

Finally, another comic reports that choosing his style evolved in part from watching the competition and from analyzing audience reaction:

> I saw that what everyone else did was generic. They were covering a lot of the same areas and not really distinguishing themselves. The people who were breaking through were similar in form but not in content. I figured that I would stay within one theme and get as deep into it as I could.
>
> When I started, I talked about a lot of themes and they got laughs, but when I talked about relationships, love, and sex, people just tuned into it and the level of response was much higher. So, I devoted myself to matters of the heart.[1]

<u>Finding a Direction for Your Act</u>

In addition to finding/refining a comic attitude, the comics indicate that at middle they began looking for a philosophy that defined what they wanted to "say" with their comedy. As comic Tim Jones describes it:

> Around middle, I struggled with, "How do I get beyond stock material,

> mundane observations, and the divorce jokes mentality?[12]

Jim Shubert describes the struggle for a middle act to create more substance as follows:

> Once you learn the basics, it's another struggle uphill. You've got to find out what you are trying to talk about. I want my stuff to be material of substance. I think humor is to make people laugh and think at the same time.
>
> Comics can be prophets. The times are changing so fast that a lot of people don't understand it. If they look at the comedian and see that he or she is having the same problem grasping life, they can say, "Hey, I'm not alone..."
>
> So, I try to help with humor. I try to make people laugh at certain situations that you really have no control over. I'm not trying to change the world; I'm just trying to give it a funny point of view.[3]

As comedienne Kathy Ladman points out, however, the comic must have a solid understanding of the craft before he can think about where to "take" his comedy and what he might contribute to the art form. Ladman observes:

> You have to get past the real basics before you can say, "Okay, I'm comfortable here. Now, what do I want to do?"
>
> It's like buying a house. I've gone through escrow, and all this other stuff; now how do I want to furnish it, really? What do I want the feeling to be in here? Before you were all worried, "Is this the right neighbor-hood for me?" But, once you are all settled in, you can own it. You can say, "Yes, I am a comedian. I deserve to be a comedian. It's the right thing for me." Then you can think, "Now, what do I really want to say with my comedy?"(35)

However, as Paul Dillery states, there are some performers who do not care about developing a philosophy:

> Some comics don't think anything about their philosophy. They just want the laughs—badly. They'll have one joke like this and another like that, and it's all mixed up, and there isn't much focus. However, such performers typically don't get beyond being a middle act.(24)

Definitions of "Good" and "Bad" Comics at Middle

As a feature act, the comics began to form more sophisticated definitions of good and bad comics. As one comic put it, "A good comic is someone who creates, someone who is prolific, and somebody who takes the art a step further." Paul Dillery observes:

> Too many guys are just imitations of imitations. A good comic is someone who is unique, someone who has different material and a different kind of character. That's hard because you have to talk about things that the audience can connect with. So, I admire anybody who can find things that are clean, that everybody can understand, and things that haven't been done to death.[24]

Comic John Roarke adds that a good comedian is someone who not only makes you laugh, but one who does some healing as well as tearing down. Rourke states:

> Lily Tomlin builds up, heals, and makes us realize our common humanity. There is an obvious love for everyone underneath her comedy. There is a benevolence throughout her work that is very healing. Comedy can take things apart, but it can put them back together. Charlie Chaplin did that. He played a tramp, but the tramp always had a lot of dignity. Underneath everything Laurel and Hardy did had the concept of camaraderie at its core.[27]

Humor is basically "truth told funny." Hence, several comics argue that the best performers are those who are able to capture *the truth of a situation* or *the essence of a character*. Some comics, like Joey Medina, argue that, "a good comic is very instinctive." For example, an "instinctive" comic works "in the moment," "feels out" the audience, can work without pre-planned material, and never does exactly the same set twice.

For many comics, great comedy has both a timeless quality and a universal appeal. For example, it has been said that much of Will Rogers' work is relevant today and that "he had his finger on the pulse of this country." Other comics cite the classic humor of the Marx Brothers as a model.

Finally, several comics assert that they especially appreciate comedians who are able to *show* as well as *tell* a joke or story. They add that the more skills the comic has and the greater his versatility, the better performer he will be. Comedian John Caponera explains:

> The more weapons you have to make people laugh, the better. Use everything at your disposal, like sound effects, voice impressions, and the way you use your body. The more things that you have in your arsenal, the more you can "sell" a joke and the funnier you're going to be. In addition, if the crowd isn't buying one shtick, you can always try another.[13]

Learning the Comic's Code of Ethics

During the middle years, comics also learned a code of ethics, i.e., what is expected of them and what will earn them respect among their peers. Jim Shubert describes several elements of the comedian's unwritten code of conduct this way:

> How do you earn respect? You do good work. You work hard. You earn the respect of other comics by showing you are not in a rush to push people aside or step on anybody. Also, you don't steal; you create. Don't work "easy." Don't come up with an easy reference. Throw two brain cells on a joke. Finally, you can't go in trying to be the funniest one. You have to give it up to the guys who have paid their dues.[3]

The theft of material is considered a violation of the comic's code of ethics. A comic whose theft is flagrant may acquire a sullied reputation. Moreover, as the following excerpt illustrates, other comics will take action against those who violate this rule frequently:

> One comic back East was stealing a lot of material. Another comic followed this comedian to another club and wrote down each piece of material that had been lifted from other comics. The comic who did the investigating then called the other comedians and informed them of the theft. When the offending comic returned, the other comics were waiting for him to do an intervention. They also called the staff of a late night entertainment program and reported the comic.

> The comic's upcoming TV appearance was subsequently cancelled.
> [Anonymous]

Developing Some Interesting Self-Images

By the feature act stage, the comics acquire interesting images of themselves. Some refer to themselves as "conquerors," "successful salesman," "bullfighters," or "a line tamer who puts his head in the lion's mouth." Bill Kalmenson, for example, states:

> We're like "top gun"—a certain breed. We are the daredevils of show business—the high wire act.[1]

Comedian Argus Hamilton likens comedians to:

- Warriors jousting with the audience.
- Foot soldiers going up on stage every night ready to die for their art.
- Gunslingers—somebody always wins in a gunfight. It's either you or the crowd.
- Saviors: "It's not easy being a savior. We make fun of anything that tries to control us, whether it is external threats to our nation, a traffic cop, or fashion dos and don'ts."

Hamilton adds: "We're like a warrior taking on an entire army [the audience], and figuring out the trickery to get to their hearts. Why? For the glory, of course."

Comic John Fox asserts that, "God gave the world 'angels' in the form of comics." Fox explains:

> My job is to walk out on stage and make sure everybody has a good time. There will probably be babies born because some of these couples will go home and make love because I did a good show. God threw me down here as an angel to make sure that people laugh and make love.[56]

Finally, comedian Vic Dunlop offers the following view of comics—as "empaths."

> Stand-up comics are the "empaths" for mankind. I believe the reason that comics can make 300 people in an audience laugh is because what the comedian is saying is what they truly feel, but which they can't voice because of religious inhibitions, social inhibitions, and political inhibitions. We comics get up there and say what we think is funny and tap into the hearts and minds of 300, 400, 2,000, or 5,000 people. That's our job. And the audience is laughing because they are saying, "He's right. I believe the same thing, and it's hilarious." They just don't have the courage to say it.[47]

Becoming a Writer

Many comics report that during the middle act phase they improved significantly as comedy writers. As a middle act, the comic is continuing to accumulate material. However, his focus is also on crafting a more polished and more versatile act suitable for the longer performances at middle and headliner. Growth as a comedy writer further includes learning to periodically review one's material, creating longer comedy routines, and learning to construct a very strong thirty-minute act.

Comedienne Diane Nichols states that at middle she developed an appreciation for the "good written joke." Nichols explains:

> A good written line means that you can do the joke over and over in different environments and in front of different people, and it works. That is much more difficult than an ad-lib, because the ad-lib can be a cheap laugh-getter and it may be done to death by other comics. There are a few ad-libs that I remember as some of my best moments on stage, but I am the most proud of something that I thought of, in my home, that I can do for an audience in Oklahoma, in California, and in Winnipeg.[4]

Learning Various Writing Techniques

As a middle act, the young comic also learns various techniques for writing. For example, he learns the value of juxtaposing concepts and actions that one would not normally expect to be connected (i.e., he learns to incorporate humor of the unexpected).[17] He also learns the value of "comic hyperbole"—exaggerating the truth just enough for the character or situation to still be believable.

Around the three- or four-year mark, the comic also learns various techniques to help spur his creativity. One comic describes the method that he used to stimulate his writing:

> I learned to list a whole page of nouns and then make a whole page of adjectives and then read the two of them to see which ones struck some sort of comedic spark in my mind. Then, I created a joke based on those two words.[21]

Comic Joey Gaynor offers the following writing advice (the 90/10 rule), which had been passed on to him by veteran comic Ed Bluestone of National Lampoon fame:

> Write out all that you have on the subject you are working on. Rule of thumb: 90 percent is junk; 10 percent is gold. Find the gold.[52]

Finally, many comics voiced a strong dislike for mediocre writing and laziness in creating material. As comic Joey Gaynor put it: "If you are going to perform on stage, have something to say." Gaynor adds:

> It doesn't have to be political, but separate yourself from the crowd. Accept the challenge to be clever and original. Be committed to the art. Voice your opinion in a funny way or just be silly—as long as it's funny. Don't waste the audience's time by

> doing nothing when it is your job to entertain.[52]

Learning to Use the Audience as a Writing Partner

In addition to formal writing techniques, the comic also learns to use the audience to create new material. Several comics indicate that they often generated material based on their interactions with audiences. As one comic describes it:

> A lot of comics write up on stage, too. They'll come up with an ad-lib or a concept on stage. In the last six months, I've come up with about five minutes of material just based on what's happened with an audience. I've had people yell things out, and then I've incorporated them into my act.[21]

Comic Joey Gaynor also recommends listening to the advice that others offer with an open ear, even if it is from someone you don't particularly like. Gaynor explains:

> Sometimes, an outsider may just see something different about you, your set, or a bit that might be helpful to you.[52]

Learning to Edit

As his writing skills improve, a smart comic will also develop his editing skills. To organize their writing and facilitate editing, many comics maintain card files or notebooks as a means of organizing their material. Other comics retain their acts on personal computers. As comic Tom Ryan recalls:

> My writing kicked up a notch when I went from jotting things down in a notebook to organizing my jokes on a word processor.[64]

As the comic learns to edit his work, Ron Richards recommends developing the discipline of "looking at your material and getting rid of the pieces that aren't you." John Wing agrees, and explains:

> You learn the value of editing out the inappropriate stuff, the stuff that is too cruel, too gross, or too inconsistent with your image. Too many guys don't realize that, or else they don't care enough to take that stuff out.[28]

Comedian Rocky LaPorte describes the approach to editing he developed this way:

> I don't like a lot of extra words. I want as many laughs per minute as I can get. So, I work hard to get the "fat" out.

Comic Tom Ryan reports, "Tightening up the joke can literally double the laugh you get." Comic John Caponera agrees and shares the following technique for editing:

> I write out every joke that I do, and then I go back and try to find where the jokes are. I gradually tighten it all up so that it's not too long in between laughs. If a joke is too long, you'd better have a big punch line.(13)

As he learns the importance of reviewing his existing material, a comic may also begin to systematically update references for older jokes. For example, if it's an older joke about game shows, the comic may substitute the name of a current game show, if appropriate.

At this stage, the comic also discovers that he must devote some time to working out the ideas for the jokes that he has been collecting. Tom Ryan illustrates:

> My problem is that I generate too much stuff. I never focus on one joke. I'll work on one bit, but then I'm generating three new ones. Then, I am overwhelmed by having a hundred new bits I want to work out, and it's like, "Where do I begin?" I find it very frustrating that I generate a lot of bits, but work out way too small a percentage.(64)

Club owner Bob Fisher points out that, "Ideally, there should be a continual process of editing your material." Fisher adds:

> There should be a process of weeding your material so that the weakest material is removed and something

> else is tried, so that eventually all the weak stuff is gone, and you only have a solid act. Then, you can headline.

Developing Sophisticated Editing Skills

As he middles, the comic learns to edit his material *while he is on stage*. One comic describes the mental editing he did during a performance this way:

> Sometimes I'm planning when I'm on stage. I'll think, "Well, this audience won't laugh at that bit which is coming up. I'll cut that out and I'll do another bit I wasn't originally going to do, because this crowd will like it."(49)

To tailor his performance, a comic may also incorporate "test jokes" into his act. Paul Dillery describes this process:

> Some comics use test jokes that they do near the beginning of their set to see whether they can do certain kinds of material. For example, I'll do some jokes to see whether I can do dark humor about funerals, death, or suicide.(24)

Comedian Jeff Cesario illustrates several other reasons the comic may need to edit his material for different types of performances during the middle years:

> There are different purposes for different sets. If there's somebody in the room I need to impress, I'm going to go with the "A" stuff. I'll do a

> set where all the nuts and bolts are tightened down. If I know that I have to run a couple sets by the Letterman people, I'll be trying to get those in shape. If what I want to accomplish is a creative thing, then that's what I'm going after during that set. If there is pacing or something else I want to work on, I work on that. Sometimes I just go up thinking, "Stay loose." I don't pre-plan anything. That helps to keep you thinking on your feet.[32]

Comedian Gary Mule Deer summarizes the importance of knowing your material and being able to edit on your feet:

> I was doing the *Tonight Show* one night, and just as the curtain was opening and I was being introduced, the stage manager said to me, "Stretch two minutes; no panel." He meant that they were short on time, and that I would not be going over to sit on the panel, but that they wanted me to do two additional minutes of monologue. In that situation, you don't have a choice; you must be able to do that.[36]

Finally, with an unappreciative audience, sometimes a comic may edit-in material for his own amusement—or in retaliation. John Wing illustrates:

> If I really hate an audience, if I think they are stupid or if they are not giv-

> ing me what I'm worth, I have certain jokes that I will do that are quite offensive. I have a sick sense of humor, and there are jokes that I won't do normally; but, if a crowd really makes me angry, I will do them. It's like, if they are not going to give me any fun, then I'm going to have my own fun.[28]

Constructing a Longer Act

In addition to mastering the finer points of writing and editing, the comic must learn how to construct a strong thirty-minute act. For example, he learns to include jokes of different lengths. Varying the length of bits helps to assure that the comic won't bore an audience with a monotonous rhythm.

The comedian also learns the value of incorporating a running gag or a recurring line into his act (e.g., Judy Tenuta's line, "It could happen!"). Frequently, the comic will also insert a joke that he will "call back" or refer to again in a few minutes. As comic John Wing describes it, "You learn to be sneaky and come at the audience from around the back." Or, to paraphrase another comic: it's always nice to come full circle and to create closure with your material.

Part of constructing a good act involves learning some basic rules about opening and closing one's performance. As one comic put it, "You want to have a *strong opening*. You want to throw the first punch to capture their attention and make sure they are listening."[5] However, you don't want a beginning that is too strong, because then you have to worry about sustaining that intensity. Fritz Coleman explains:

> You want the opening to be good because you want the audience to like you, to trust you, and to think, "Hey, he's funny. I'll listen to what he has to say." You also want to do character-revealing material up-front so that they get to know who you are and what your comedy is about right away.[15]

Although most comics like to "open strong," there are some exceptions. Some comics like to build slowly and work toward the end. Other comics like to be daring and may open with new material.[24] However, as John Roarke notes:

> Whether you open strong or not depends on who you are and what you are doing. It also depends on what works for you, what you want to achieve, and how you feel.[27]

The comics also indicate that you want to put your strongest material toward the end of your act. It is an old vaudeville tradition to "close strong" so that the audience will go away thinking, "Hey, he was good." As one comic described it, you want to close big so that you get your due (applause), and so they pay attention to the next act.[5] Therefore, tradition and showmanship require that the comic "always leave them laughing."

One comedienne reports that after about three and a half years, she "finally came up with a 'killer close.'" She explains the importance of a very strong closing routine this way:

> Even if they hated me before, when I do my closing routine, they scream. It always works, and I get to go off to applause.[8]

Once the comic has anchored his act with strong opening material and a great closer, some comics recommend that you try to build toward the middle. Other performers like to construct a beginning, middle, and end for their act. Several comics also report that as you construct your act, it is important to have a show that is *well-paced*, i.e., ideally, the comic wants his act to have peaks and valleys. Comic Tim Jones illustrates:

> At middle, I learned that I had to let them rest. I was hitting them with so many jokes that I was tiring them out. So, I had to slow down, throw in a longer story, and then get rolling again for a little while.[12]

One comic likens the crafting of an act to the creation of a symphony: one may include all the nuances including rests, stops, and crescendos. Paul Provenza describes how he viewed constructing a longer act:

> Around middle, you start to think in terms of Gestalt [the whole] instead of just individual pieces. When I was a middle, I tried to find a "through line" in my material. I took all the scattered

> things that I was doing and tried to find a way to put them together so they had a beginning, a middle, and an end. I tried to figure it out thematically. The theme or through line told me that this bit belonged here or that this bit should precede that one. Then, when I moved something around, I thought, "Now, how do I get from here to there?". That was fertile ground for a bridge that I needed to create. I've always respected the art form, and that's why I try to visualize structure, and that's why I try to put so many layers into my writing.[37]

Having a well-paced act becomes even more important when the comic must do a longer show as a headliner. Therefore, the attention to the organization and the pacing of his material at this stage prepares the comic to headline.

Honing the Technical Aspects of Performing

As a middle act, the comic typically discovers that he must grow as a performer. For example, Tim Jones observes, "Although I might have 'bluffed' my way through twenty minutes with lots of audience interaction as an opening act, as a middle act I discovered that I needed to develop a more versatile performance."[12] Jones explains:

> As an opener, I could ad lib for a long time. Then, I ran into a Friday, second show audience who didn't want to talk. They didn't respond to my ask-

> ing "What do you do? Where are you from?" These people were tired, and they just came to see a show. They didn't want to be involved; they just wanted to watch, and I was stuck. Ten minutes into it, I realized, "Oh, God, I can't talk to them." I found out that you had to have material, so that if they want to talk, you can talk. If they don't want to talk, you do your material.[12]

In addition to being able to go back and forth between talking to the audience and doing his material, the comic must learn to adjust the pace of his act for different audiences. Tim Jones explains:

> In Hawaii and in the South, the pace of life is much slower. They listen slower—they really do. They don't have to digest information as fast as they do in New York. So, you have to wait four or even five seconds to let them get the joke.[12]

As a feature act, the comic also learns to adjust his material to particular performing venues. John Wing describes one approach the middle comic might take as he plays a broader array of venues:

> If it's a bar and it doesn't do comedy regularly, talk real loud, talk fast, swear a lot, and don't pause in between. Don't give them a chance. If they heckle you, get bigger. You need

> a much bigger presence when they are rowdy. You can't ever let them have the last word, because they're like dogs. They'll eat you. They will. I've seen it happen. So, you must establish that you belong on stage.(28)

Wing adds that, with experience, the comic learns:

> In some situations, the age of your audience will guide you in choosing your material. In other cases, if you know the other comics, you'll know what should be working. That can help you adjust your set. You'll know if the audience is easily offended, if you can do your clever stuff, and if they read the newspaper. Ideally, you want your act to appeal to a broad spectrum of people, and you want very slight adjustments in any situation.(28)

By this stage, the comic has learned small tricks that help to make him a better performer. For example, *making eye contact* with an audience member can be helpful when it comes to connecting with the crowd. Dan Smith explains how comics learn to use their eyes:

> If you look at an audience member in the eye while you are telling your joke, they think that you are talking just to them. You are drawing them in. There is a noticeable difference when you engage people rather than looking at the floor or the "fourth wall."

> Some theatrical comics perform for this imaginary wall of faces instead of looking at the audience right in the eye. But, I think that singling out one or two audience members conveys that I'm not just walking through my act. It also gives the illusion that everything is coming off the top of my head, even when it's not.(61)

During this stage, the comic's timing and his ability to play off of the audience's reaction also become more finely honed. John Wing illustrates how comics learn to use their ears:

> Often, up there on stage you can't see a single face. I'm just sucking laughs from a black hole. It's all sound. After a while, you learn to feel the sound, to feel the laugh. And you've got to know when it's going to end. The laugh comes up, you hear it, and you decide how intense it is going to be. Just as it starts to drop off, you have to be right there with the next joke.(28)

Comic Billy Gardell states that as a feature act, one performing skill he learned was how to "work the pockets." Gardell explains:

> You deliver the set-up to the left side and the punch line in the middle. Then, you deliver a set-up in the middle and a punch line to the right side. Then, you deliver a set-up to the right

> and a punch to the left. That way, you unify the room. Then, it's a matter of keeping eye contact with all three pockets so you hold their attention.[65]

As a middle act, the comic also strengthens his ability to *recreate his material consistently.* Comic John Roarke explains:

> You have to be a little bit of an actor. You have to be able to enter into the "scene." You enter into the joke as you would enter into a scene, and you do that as if it were for the first time. You enter into that moment, so that you're not simply reciting words that you've memorized. You have to let the imaginary circumstances of a joke impact you so that you're creating it anew.[27]

Comic Nick Gaza agrees and states, "The real skill in telling a joke is performing it so well that the audience thinks you just thought of it then and there." Eddie Merrill adds:

> It's very hard to do something the same way each time and to make it like it's the first time it's been done. You get tired. One of the most difficult aspects of comedy is making it fresh each time. But, the audience lets you know whether you have that ability or not.[21]

Finally, it is as a middle act that the comic learns his performing strengths. Rocky LaPorte illustrates:

> Some guys have good timing. Some guys are good "salesmen." Dennis Wolfberg had great timing. George Wallace "sells" jokes you wouldn't think would be funny with a great big smile. I think my strong point is editing. But, it takes time to learn that.(42)

Defining and Managing "Off" Nights

By the time he is a middle act, the comic is able to draw on his expanding joke file and his performing experience to put on a good show most of the time. However, as Eddie Merrill explains, "As consistent as a comic may become, he can never be entirely confident about a joke." Merrill adds, "Comedy is never an exact science" and explains:

> No matter what joke you think is going to kill in every situation, there's going to come a time when that joke will "eat it." It's not the strength of the joke. It's not the delivery. It's not the timing. It's not the audience. It's the whole combination of things. One night, the timing, the pace, and the wording will kill. It will be great. It will work perfectly. It will fit for that audience and for that performance. The next night with a similar crowd, in a similar club, it's delivered in the same way, and you get—nothing. You just go "Gosh."(21)

However, by the fourth year, even on the bad nights, the comic can now better differentiate the reasons for having had a bad show. Although bombing may still hurt, the comic can legitimately define a slow set as "having an off night." Eddie Merrill explains:

> You may be one or two beats away from the big laugh. You might get little laughs and not really be bombing, but you're not really being expressive of your character. You may be downplaying things, or you may choose not to maneuver the show to get a particular person interested or to get the group that's talking back.(21)

When he bombs at this stage, Merrill reports that the comedian may not feel well or he may have had something traumatic happen. The comic also may not make a connection with the audience and/or he doesn't understand what the audience wants. Finally, as Merrill sums it up:

> The comic may be unwilling to give the audience what it wants. They're going to do what they do, and that is all there is to it—whether the audience is entertained or not that night. I guess every comic, at one time or another, falls into all of these categories.(21)

Reading and Managing Audiences

The comic's worst nightmare is that the crowd will turn on him. To combat this fear, the comedian learns sophisticated methods of controlling the audience. In order to establish control, the comic refines his skills for "reading" audiences. As one comic describes it:

> Reading an audience becomes second nature, but you're not really aware of the process. It's all in the size of the room and the kind of feelings you get from the audience. It's all a sensation. I don't really think it's something you can teach somebody. It's just something you feel the audience out for. It is just an awareness that you develop.
>
> Most of the time if you're good, you make the decision correctly. Sometimes you're wrong. Sometimes you go in one direction and it's wrong, and you have to be able to recover from it. Only your best comics can read all audiences.[21]

There are also times when the ability to read the audience may be less important than others. Eddie Merrill explains:

> If you are playing certain clubs all the time, you learn what the house attracts. In that situation, the ability to read audiences may not be as important. Once you know a room, you don't have to worry as much about what they are going to be like.
>
> Some comedians never learn to read an audience well, and it is to

> their detriment. Other comics never learn it and it doesn't seem to matter. For some reason their charisma carries them. They can basically do anything and the audience will love them. Those comics don't have to worry as much about reading an audience.[21]

If a comic can't get a handle on a crowd, he is likely to go ahead with his act and hope that it will catch. As one comic reports, "You think, 'Well, I'll just do what I do.' A lot of comics call that 'putting it on autopilot.'"[21]

Learning Advanced Heckler Skills

At middle, the comic also learns how to handle hecklers with greater ease. At the feature stage, a comic learns that some kinds of hecklers even help a show by providing him with an opening to perform something funny from his joke file. If they are not too disruptive, hecklers can also add variety and bring a dynamic quality to the comic's performance.

With experience, the comic learns that he must get the audience on his side and not on the heckler's.[5] To do this, many comics use some variation of the following request for silence: "This crowd has paid a cover charge to see a comedy show. They've also paid good money for food and drinks. They did not pay to hear you yell things. Please be quiet."

The comic also learns to identify audience members who are likely to heckle. Larry Omaha calls audience members who yell things out in agreement with the comic, "accidental" hecklers who mean no harm. Another comic describes several other types of hecklers:

> First, there is the very hostile guy who's just bummed out on life. Down deep he's a frustrated comic, but he knows he hasn't got the balls. He wants to prove to you and to the audience that he's funnier than you are.
>
> A second type of heckler is just a guy who's having a good time and he wants to play. He's the most fun because he understands that this is his part and you can have a give and take with him. He also knows when the play time is over.
>
> The third type is the kind that bothers me the most. They are the ones who have no respect for anybody who isn't "somebody." Their attitude is, "I don't know who you are. I paid my money to see the star." They are very crass and they are basically telling you, "Hey, get off the stage; you're wasting my time."(2)

Some comics develop their own policies for dealing with hecklers. Eddie Merrill describes his "three heckle rule" this way:

> If you get heckled once, you put the heckler down. If you get heckled again, you put them down again. If

> they heckle you a third time, and the management hasn't done anything, you let them win; but you let them win only in their own eyes, so that the audience knows that you are giving it up. That usually shuts them up. If they are still going to heckle, you make some gesture or signal to the management that you don't want that element in the room.[21]

Heckling and performance interruptions are a part of the job. Having a beer bottle or a lit pack of matches thrown at you represent the difficult part of performing. Along with "slow" sets they are a hazard with which the comic must learn to live. For example, comic Argus Hamilton states that the comic must develop the ability to weather the ebb and flow of audience reaction. He explains:

> You get such a thick hide after a while that it takes a pretty big situation to make you feel that bad. A bad set at a small club doesn't bother me. A slow set on the *Tonight Show* would bother me. A slow set in Las Vegas would bother me because I know the money is on the line there.[17]

Another comic describes coming to the realization that a mix of shows is normal:

> Once you are doing comedy for a few years, you realize that *a mix of good and bad shows is somehow typical*. Even when you have a great

> show, that's as false as having a bad show; it usually falls in the middle somehow.[39]

In sum, when a comic can go on stage, handle a heckler with aplomb, turn the energy in a crowd around, and make the performance "look" easy, therein exists the "art" of stand-up. These are also among the key skills that are mastered during the middle act phase.

Learning the Business Aspects of Show Business

As a feature act, the comic learns that "show business" consists of two words—show and business. As comic Tim Jones points out:

> You tend to learn about the business at middle because as an opening act, you've just walked into the garden, and you are still just seeing all the flowers. You're amazed by all the flowers. As a middle, you learn that these flowers need work. You learn that someone's got to take care of them. Somebody's got to water them and make them grow. You learn that someone's got to keep strangers off the property.[12]

At middle, the comic learns what the important business issues are and how to attend to them. He also learns that if either the "show" or the "business" part is lacking, the performer will have a problem.

Diane Nichols sums up the comic's business concerns at middle this way:

> At three to four years, you're concerned about upping your money, getting more "prestige" gigs, getting TV exposure, and moving from middle to headliner.[4]

Bill Kalmenson describes the comic's business concerns at the feature act stage in the following terms:

- How do I break away from the pack?
- How do I get what I'm worth on the road?
- How do I deal more effectively with bookers?
- How do I deal with owners so that I am treated more fairly?
- How do I keep my calendar full?[1]

Often, other comics are an important source of information about the business. For example, comics tend to cluster at comedy clubs. While waiting in the green room or standing outside the club, a young comic can learn from his fellow performers how to negotiate salary, which clubs pay well, and which clubs are "dives."

As a middle act, the comic also learns about the importance of public relations. For example, the comic learns about the process of sending out clips, creating a Website, and putting together a press kit containing a "head shot" (photograph), his television/performing credits, and favorable publicity he has received.

In addition, at middle the comic learns about the importance of networking and keeping in touch with people. He also learns about making the connections necessary for television exposure. As one comic phrased it, "You learn to schmooze."

Connecting with an Agent/Manager

At the middle stage, many of the comics did not yet have agents or managers who represented them. A few comics said they weren't ready for an agent yet. Several comics spoke of the difficulty in finding a good agent. Some state that "if you're lucky" or "when the time is right," you connect with someone. Other comics liken the process of finding an agent to dating: the right chemistry should be there.

Several comics also suggest that it is much better to wait for an agent to approach them than for the comic to approach someone. The logic one comic offers for this tack is that if the agent approaches the comic, it indicates that he sees something in the comic, and he is more likely to do a better job of representing him.

Beginning to Develop a Following

After several years of performing, the comic develops a following among audiences and he builds a reputation with owners that he is reliable. Fritz Coleman states that both factors can play an important role in convincing owners to let the comic move into headlining. Coleman explains:

> The latter part of your experience as a middle, you start to be a draw: people see you, like you, and they come back to see you. When you're a headliner, your job is to "put people's butts in seats." So, the latter part of being a middle, you start to develop a following.
>
> There are some guys who can headline in certain parts of the country who can only middle in other parts of the country because they haven't endeared themselves or proven themselves to club owners.
>
> However, if you get a *Tonight Show* credit *and* you can benefit the club by bringing more people to the club, then you can headline more easily.[15]

As they waited for their first television spot, some comics report that they began to avoid excessively violent references and eliminate jokes that rely on company names. They started to avoid jokes that are "hacky," and began to focus on their own original material. These steps prepare the comic to work "clean" on network television. Such editing also provides the flexibility the comic needs to work other jobs that require a clean performance (e.g., entertaining at certain corporate meetings).

Getting Your First Television Exposure

At four or five years, many comics become increasingly impatient for their "big break." Television exposure is sought after and holds the key to the comic's next career level. Appearing on Leno or Letterman provides the comic with national exposure *and* credibility with club owners and audiences. Tom Ryan, for example, recalls:

> Getting my first Letterman was the most nerve-wracking experience and the most exhilarating five minutes of my life. That moment changed my overall level of confidence, and it's a part of my career that you can't take away. It came at a point in my career where I was starting to get burned out, and it rejuvenated my enthusiasm. I got back into writing new material and planning. It also helped me with the corporate circuit: corporate clients will watch my tapes now. With TV credits, doors that are closed will open a little more easily when you knock on them.[64]

There is also another level of learning that occurs as the comic begins to perform on TV. Comedian Darryl Sivad explains:

> TV provides a strange new pressure. The first time you do TV is like the first time you do stand-up. Now, you're introduced to a lot of light when you are used to performing in a darker room. You've got audiences much further back. You have TV cameras, and you have to take cues. You have to watch the stage manager. He is giving you signals you may not be

> familiar with. And, you must get through your act very successfully.[59]

In addition to conferring professional status, television exposure increases the amount a comic can negotiate for club performances. With television credits, comics may jump from earning $800 per week to $2,000 per week. Without TV exposure, the comic is likely to remain working in the clubs as a feature act for lower compensation.

A smart comic will also spend some of his time in the media centers of Los Angeles or New York to be sure that he is seen by, and remains in front of, industry executives. The downside for the comic is that instead of earning the higher salaries he can command on the road, the comic will struggle with the low wages of the showcase clubs on the coasts.

Talent coordinators periodically monitor the progress of East Coast and West Coast comedians by visiting the major comedy clubs. Darryl Sivad, for example, recalls that he was "discovered" when the talent coordinator of the *Tonight Show* came to a club to review another comic, saw his act, and invited him to appear on the show. However, it is more often the case that the talent coordinator has seen or heard about a comic and will then follow the comic's progress until they feel the comic is "ready."

Until one is "discovered," however, a good portion of the comic's experience as a feature act is spent working on the road.

<u>Working the Road</u>

Most comics first go out on the road when they begin working as a middle act. (The pay is too low, in most cases, to work the road as an opening act and most clubs use local talent to open their shows). Like actors, many comics like the excitement and adventure offered by the road. Many also relish the fact that they can avoid the "9 to 5 grind." Some comics spend a great deal of time on the road. Comic John Wing, for example, once spent 282 days working on the road during one year, and 308 days on the road the next year. Other comics prefer not to travel and do so only on a much more limited basis. Whether the comedian travels a lot or a little, the road circuit is where two precious commodities for the comedian are found: stage time and money.

Jobs in comedy clubs across the country represent an opportunity to get the stage time the comic needs to experiment, refine his skills, and develop in front of diverse audiences. As one comic put it, "The road can really make you work, if you work rather than play."[39] Another comic observes:

> There is nothing like working thirty out of forty-five nights to make you sharp. A couple of long stretches like that can really help you progress.[28]

Still another comic describes the "workout" the road permits this way:

> If you go to a club where the show goes from Tuesday to Saturday, two shows on Friday night, and two on Saturday night, that's seven shows in a row. That's a lot of stage time. It just gets you honed.[39]

Comedian Jason Stuart points out, "Doing that many shows in a week, in the same room, with the same amount of time, *provides consistency and it builds your confidence*."[60] Comic Jimmy Burns adds that the road also offers the comedian a helpful perspective on good and bad performances. He states:

> If you only go up a couple times a month, the bad sets can linger. When you are doing seven shows in a week, the bad sets don't carry as much weight and it puts the good shows in perspective as well.[39]

In addition to helping the comic develop his skills, road gigs represent a major source of income. As one comic observes, "It's a good moment when you can actually survive on comedy alone." Comedienne Valerie Pappas adds:

> When you can finally support yourself doing comedy, it's a reason to be grateful—even on the bad nights. You think to yourself, "Well, it could be worse. I could be doing a job I really hate."[38]

Coming to the realization that he is making more money doing comedy than he ever made at any of his other jobs also reinforces the comic's confidence in his ability, and it strengthens his identity as a professional.

Working on the road represents a maturing experience for those comics who had not previously traveled much. More importantly, traveling introduces the comics to a wide variety of people and places—two commodities with which they would need to be familiar in order to discuss human nature on stage. As comic John Caponera describes it:

> I really started to grow when I worked on the road. I got a better perspective of what people were all about, and what life was like outside of the South Side of Chicago. I figured that if I was going to make everyone laugh, I had to travel and find out what's going on in the country. The American South is different than the Midwest. The Midwest is different than the East Coast, and the East Coast is different than Los Angeles.(13)

Comedienne Diane Nichols describes the benefits that working on the road had for her this way:

> When I fly into a new city and go out to grocery shop for the week, I feel like I've had a chance to really see this country and to live in little neighborhoods all over the United States.(4)

Dan Smith recalls the growth that the road provided this way: "I turned my strong thirty minutes of material into a decent forty-five, and then into a stronger forty-five. Then, I built it up to an hour of material." Smith also reflects:

> Of course, I grew at the expense of fifty people in small clubs in small cities on the road. In all comics' ca-

> reers, somebody's got to suffer! I've watched people walk out on the best comics. That has to happen at some point because nobody kills every night for their whole career. Some audience has to suffer at some point for your own growth.(61)

Sometimes, the road offers a solitude that is useful for writing. As comic Nick Gaza observes: "When you are alone, it forces you to look at others and yourself more."

Traveling also provides the comic with the confidence that his material will work in different settings.(26, 12) As one comic describes it, "You start to say, 'Oh, it worked in Tucson. It worked in Colorado Springs. I guess my material really does work!'"... Then I realized, "It was not just a 'good room'-I was *funny*. Things went well because I was funny."(39)

Working on the road also means that the comic is surrounded by other comics and has an opportunity to learn about the craft from them. As one comic explains:

> You hang out with the other comics. You listen and you learn how to use your writing muscle. I'd surround myself with some of the funniest guys I know—and that's a very strong force. If you've got nine guys working on a joke, you can't help but come up with seven funny references.

The comics also spoke about another aspect of road life that helped them with their separation from family and friends:

Comics often create "family" bonds with other comics. As Diane Nichols describes it:

> I walk into a condo, and I am looking at two guys I've never laid eyes on before. We're in different bedrooms, but we're rooming together, and we become a family for one week. We go to the movies. We go out to eat. We scream at each other. But, at the same time, after many years, what means the most to me is the respect of my peers. It's not an easy job. And, when you wake up alone in Saskatchewan and you miss the guys and the camaraderie, you find that that becomes the backbone of what matters to you.(4)

Other comics also help newer guys to deal with problems they encounter when traveling. Some of the major problems the comics report having on the road include:

- Getting decent accommodations.
- Being booked in clubs that are dives.
- Being booked in places that are totally incompatible with their act.
- Learning to fight for fair pay.
- Learning how to handle situations in which they are cheated.

- Learning how to use their time off-stage effectively.

Kathy Buckley describes the difficulty a comic can have learning to use his money wisely on the road:

> It's very easy to spend money on the road. Even though you may be put up in a comedy condo, you can use a lot of money just buying food every day. I would go into the condos and ask the guys if they wanted to chip in. I offered to buy the groceries, and we cooked our meals. I wanted to come home with my money, not spend it all.[63]

Another major task for comics is learning to deal with the loneliness on the road in a way that is not self-destructive. Diane Nichols illustrates how lonely the road can be:

> You're in a strange place among strangers. Sometimes, I stay in the fetal position all day in my hotel bed and watch the soap operas. I'm not going on until 8:00 or 9:00 p.m. I'm in a distant city, like Saskatchewan. It's snowing. I can't leave the hotel. I watch TV and wait for the next meal.
>
> In the beginning, it's like you are playing hooky and it's fun. But, some gigs they don't hang out with you after the show. The local comics have their own lives, and they leave the minute

> they get off stage. The owner has split. You're sent home in a cab, and you are there all alone. It can be very lonely.
>
> Even the men watch the soap operas. It's the one thing that's there whether you are in North Carolina or Sacramento.[4]

John Caponera agrees, and adds:

> The road is the saddest part of the business. You're getting all this love and acceptance on stage; then, a few minutes later, you're alone in your hotel room, eating a pizza, and watching HBO; the loneliest guy in the world. Living on the road is not a good life. You grow old real quick. You don't have a life. You're like a nomad, traveling from town to town, living out of a suitcase.[13]

Even the comics who enjoy working on the road concede that road life exacts a very high price. However, as one comic put it, "reading, writing, making calls, networking, and pursuing business contacts in nearby cities can all help to counter the difficulties of road life."[39]

Club owners also can make life on the road difficult. Some owners provide accommodations that are filthy, run-down, or otherwise unfit for humans (e.g., crusty towels, doors with no locks, etc.)[66] Kathy Buckley provides the following example:

> One of the first things I learned, early on, was to bring my own sheets and towels to the comedy condos. When I walked into one early gig and saw the bed, I said, "I'm flipping this mattress over." It was disgusting.[63]

The comics also complain that the owners of some clubs are just businessmen pushing liquor, and some don't care about anyone or the art form. Some owners do not pay fair wages; others have been known to "offer drugs instead of money for a gig."[4, 12]

On the other hand, a number of comics acknowledge that there is a lot of 'flotsam and jetsam' among the ranks of comics in the business. They admit that club owners have had some justified complaints about crude and destructive behavior on the part of some comics in the comedy condos. As one comic put it, "Some of the guys are scum, and they give the rest a bad reputation."[4] These so-called "fun monkeys" have been known to "drink up a storm," try to score with all the waitresses in every city, and damage club property.

The comics also report that you can get lazy, work dirty, and let your creative juices dry-up on the road. Moreover, when the comic is traveling he is not making industry connections, and he does not have visibility in the entertainment industry centers of New York and Los Angeles. As one comic put it, "Sometimes, you feel like you don't want to be out of town in case a booker stops by the club."[5] John Caponera also observes:

> You can work the road clubs until you are blue in the face, and you'll

> always work for the same price. Unless you have television exposure, you can never be a draw. But, you've got comics who just work the road. They don't have apartments. They live out of their cars and go from gig to gig.(13)

Comic John Caparulo cautions that road warriors can become accustomed to performing in smaller cities for audiences who will laugh at anything. They may also rely on props or stock material that will not be successful with audiences in New York or Los Angeles. Finally, Caparulo notes that a road comic also may become used to performing for thirty to forty-five minutes. These comics can become very frustrated when they encounter judgmental audiences on the coasts and when they do not get the same stage time in the New York or Los Angeles clubs as they did on the road.

Finally, K.T. Tatara adds the following advice for middle comics working the road:

> Most of the time when you go out on the road you are on your own. You have to do it all yourself. You book yourself. No one is looking after you. You have to take it upon yourself to record your sets, watch or listen to your recordings, and analyze them so you can get better. Yes, you get to go to a local restaurant, sightsee, and meet a lot of different people. That's fun; but, you have to remember the work part. Otherwise, you are never going to move forward.

> Some people learn to work hard, and some people party too much. I think every comedian has had friends who have gone on the road and it just got the best of them. Could be alcohol or drugs, or they just didn't do the work. They were funny and talented, but they didn't have the discipline to look after themselves. You must use the road as your training ground for the big stages. You need to see the bigger picture. Eventually, you want to develop an act that gets on HBO. Therefore, every night counts.(99)

Confronting the Demons and Managing Time Off Stage

Alcohol is an integral part of the comedy club setting. Drugs are typically within easy reach. Hence, the lure of these substances can be a *very* serious problem for some comics. Frequent use of drugs or alcohol abuse can result in an inability to pay one's rent. In addition, one's electricity or phone may be turned off. Or, as comedian Vic Dunlop describes it, "There are sex stories, scandalous stories, drug stories, hooker stories, and much more."

The fact that comics spend twenty-three hours a day *off* stage also provides another major challenge for them. As comedian Argus Hamilton observes:

> The comic's most serious problem is the time they spend off stage. I think that the difference between success and stagnation is the way you take care of yourself off stage. Most of us spent our twenties unsuccessfully trying

> to kill ourselves. During the next couple decades we look at ourselves and figure it's time to do something with our lives. When we reach that moment of responsibility, then I think our careers will take off. Guys who take off before that, take off too soon. They haven't made the decision to commit their lives to their work and not to the next buzz.[17]

Day jobs such as radio disc jockey, the responsibilities of parenthood, the joys of grandparenthood, and avocations such as golf or playing competitive tennis can sometimes help the comic to maintain balance. Acting and writing can also provide a stabilizing force and become a positive part of the comic's identity. Sometimes, it takes maturity, life experience, or learning the hard way for some comics to mellow. Comic Jimmy Burns offers the following example of this maturation effect:

> One time in Indianapolis, a bunch of us comics were hanging out. The younger guys were like, "Hey, let's go party!" The older comics were like, "Nah. Been there, done that. We're playing Scrabble."[39]

In other cases, problems with drug and alcohol abuse result in a tragic outcome for comedians. Comic John Fox describes the difficulties that many comics face:

> God gave us comics a great gift to make people laugh. But, the thing is

> that if you look at Red Skelton's clown pictures, they all have tears; the tears of a clown. Every clown has a sad face because he knows that he is the life of the party for one hour—and then he goes back to his hotel room alone, watches ESPN, and wishes he had someone to hold.
>
> Everyone else gets to laugh, have fun, then go home and make love to their partner. This job ruins relationships, and the comic either turns himself into a drug addict or an alcoholic. [Just look at the list of comedians we've lost.]
>
> The funniest human beings in the world are often the most miserable. They all suffer from the same disease—loneliness. Rodney Dangerfield said it best, "It's not easy being me." That pretty much says it for all of us. I love what I do, and I wouldn't do anything else. But, as much fun as everybody thinks it is, our job has major drawbacks. God gave the rest of the world angels (comics), but we comics all suffer because of our work.(56)

Preparing to Headline (a.k.a., "Headline Fever")

By the four- or five-year mark, most middle comics are eager to headline. However, as one comic put it, "Too many comics think it is easy to headline, and they think they are ready to headline before they actually are." Comic John Wing explains:

> Everybody who middles goes around saying, "Man, I should be headlining. I don't understand why he won't headline me." Many middlers don't understand that there is a big difference between thirty minutes of consistency and forty-five minutes that gets funnier as you go along—plus the polish. It's a huge gap. It's at least as big as "no material to thirty minutes." *Rule of thumb: however long it took you to middle, that's how long it should take you to go from middle to headliner.*(28)

Comedian Rudy Moreno further reflects "in order to headline, *you must be a good entertainer, as well as a very good middle act.*"Moreno explains:

> To headline, you must be able to keep the excitement there. If you are not an adept middler, the energy in the room will be lost for the headliner. If the headliner goes up and has to work twice as hard, you won't work with him again. Before you headline, you must be able to keep the excitement there for your entire set.(43)

John Wing cautions middle comics that making the transition to headliner can be difficult. He states:

> God, it's hard to headline without credits. It's hard to convince people that you are able to do it. Bookers and owners have their prejudices, and if you appeal to them that particular day, you'll be all right. If not, it's hard to crack them. It can be very difficult to move to headliner.[(28)]

Comic Alonzo Bodden recommends that the feature comic should do *different sets* for the owner/booker *with his material* (i.e., without a lot of audience interaction), in order to showcase his versatility and demonstrate to the owner his readiness to headline.

To move up to being an "A" club headliner, the young comic *must also demonstrate his readiness to headline to his peers.* John Fox explains:

> Developing into an "A" club headliner isn't going to happen overnight. You also have to earn the respect of the "A" club *comics* for them to let you into their club. If you are doing a "hack job," you are not going to have fun. Nobody is going to like you. Once you make it to the major leagues, you had better make sure that the boys in the major leagues know that you are ready—because we will not respect you if you aren't ready.[(55)]

Comic Rocky LaPorte recommends that the comic should take his time to headline because "first impressions count." LaPorte recalls:

> I know a couple of friends of mine who wanted to headline early and they weren't ready. Then, they never got that chance again for a long time. You can only be "new" once. It's better to be ready than raw, because that's how they'll remember you.[42]

Comic Billy Gardell agrees, and adds, "One bad impression, and you may never work at a particular club again."

Comedian John Caparulo further cautions the over-eager middler, "It's hard when you are a new headliner and nobody knows you." He explains:

> [When you are a new headliner], you're the headliner, but you're not; you're just the last comic. If you are Chris Rock or Jerry Seinfeld, the audience's attention is locked in. But, when the headliner is somebody they don't know, they think, "I'm drunk anyway, let's talk."

Comedienne Tammy Pescatelli adds, "You may sell out a show once. But, if you are not funny and if you are not prepared to headline, people won't come back to see you. You have a responsibility to your fans to be ready."[66]

Comic Steve Altman offers the following advice to middlers regarding the transition to headlining:

> Take your time middling, because the middle spot is the *best* spot on the bill. The *best* spot. I'm a headliner and I *love* to middle. You get to do your best thirty minutes, and there is no pressure to be the funniest one on the bill. Enjoy that![51]

Jim Shubert observes that, typically, "When you are ready to headline, you will know it." He states:

> You'll hit a plateau. You start to realize your own self-worth. You'll feel it in yourself. You'll say, "I'm as good as anybody. I'll go head-to-head with anyone, now."[3]

Dan Smith agrees and adds:

> I think every performer remembers that point at which they were either doing as well as or better than the headliner. All it takes is that one show, and you realize that you just had a better set than the headliner. You think, "It's time. I know I'm ready to headline now."[61]

<u>Barbara's "Take" on the Middle Act Phase</u>

As a feature act, the comic reaches a place of comfort where he knows who he is as a comedic performer. He has honed and polished an act that demonstrates variety and sophistication. He knows what to do with the space on stage and he has developed confidence in his performing abilities. He is able to talk easily with the audience and he has learned techniques to firmly establish and maintain control of the crowd. He also has learned how to use audience composition and energy to his performing advantage. By the time he headlines, the middle comic also has achieved a confidence that he is able to handle *anything* that happens on stage.

In sum, the middle act phase is a "cushioned" period that allows the comic to develop his persona, to polish his act, and refine each of the skills he will need in order to headline. It is a growth period. Working on the road provides the exposure to diverse audiences that the comic will need in order to entertain whatever audience is before him. In addition, the feature act stage also offers additional experience with the performing venues, stages, and sound systems with which the comic must be comfortable. Finally, as a middle act, the comic develops a commitment to his craft. He forges a solid bond with his comic peers and, by the time he headlines, he has developed a sense of himself as a professional.

CHAPTER 5

"I'm a Comic!"

One night, on the road, you'll be tired and restless, and wonder if you made the best career choice. Then, someone will come up to you, eyes bright and shining, and say that you made them feel better. That's the night you'll realize, as a professional comic, it's all about the audience, and not your own feelings. You'll stand taller and proudly say, "I'm a comic and I make people laugh."

Diane Nichols

MOST EMBARRASSING MOMENTS

Can You Spell Mortified?

I had just finished my set, and there was a guy in the audience who was deaf. He could read lips as long the comic was looking right at him. He was laughing at the right time if the comic was looking his way, but then every once and a while when the comic turned away, he would turn to the person next to him and say, "What did he say?" Right off the bat, the audience knew he was hard of hearing. However, the second to the last comic on the line-up had not been in the room, at all, during the show. So, he starts doing his act and the deaf man in the audience turns to his friend and asks, "What did he say?" And the comic said, "Dude, what are you, deaf?" And the man said, "Yes, I am." Well, the comic literally grabbed his heart; I thought he was going to have a heart attack then and there. He collapsed on the bar stool behind him and turned purple. You could tell that this guy just wanted to die.

- Lou Santini

Always Check Your Zipper!

I was hosting a show at Stand-Up New York in New York City. I came out and as soon as I stepped on the stage the crowd was laughing. It seemed like all I had to do was say, "Hi how are you guys doing?" and they were cheering. I thought, "Wow, this crowd is hot." So, I did my first joke. I didn't think it was that great, but they roared. I said, "You guys are a pretty giggly bunch." Then, one lady in the front row pointed and gestured at me. I thought she was trying to heckle me, and I said, "What are you, Helen Keller?" and I looked down and my shirt was coming through my zipper. I just stopped, turned around, zipped up, and I said, "Well, I guess that joke worked. I hope you liked my opening bit."

- Anonymous

When You're Sick, Try Not to Laugh

One night I was performing, and I had a cold. Someone in the audience had a very funny heckler response. I started to laugh, and this glob of snot came out. It ran down and off my face before I could even do anything. It seemed like it was like in slow motion. I mean, it almost reached the floor before it let go of my nose. Only about a third of the crowd saw it, but those who did were in hysterics. I felt so embarrassed. I just apologized to everyone who saw it. It was so disgusting that people thought it was a prop; they literally thought that I had jammed something up my nose before the show.

- Anonymous

Remember That the Second Microphone Is Live!

One time, a prominent comedienne was on stage. She had eaten a burrito earlier and suddenly felt the urge to release some gas. She knew there was a big laugh coming up in her act, and figured she would sneak the gas out during the big laugh. When the laugh came she moved toward the back of the stage, but she forgot that the back-up microphone was "on" and she had inadvertently moved close to the back-up mic. So, the whole audience heard her release the gas, which was then amplified over the sound system.

- John Fox

CHAPTER 5

Comedy's a Community ...

Once admitted, you become a part of the family. An owner might bail a comic out of jail or put a performer in a drug/alcohol rehabilitation program. Owners will act as brokers for jobs if someone calls them and needs a comedian.

Comedians will attend another comic's wedding. They will inquire about a comic's sick mother or father. They will stage a benefit for another comic whose life has been touched by the serious illness of a spouse. Comics will grieve the loss of a colleague.

Comics cluster at comedy clubs and tap into a strong industry grapevine to share the latest industry news and gossip. They share information about clubs, bookers, and deals. They catch up with old friends, celebrate successes, and commiserate over bad gigs.

Veteran comics will offer advice to talented newcomers, and they will even give up a little stage time so that a young performer can develop. Many comedians provide helpful feedback for other comics.

There are comic friends with whom a comedian will write, exchange ideas, compare notes, "talk shop," and travel. These friends form a network and become an extended "family."

... But, It's Also Competitive

Some comics are ambitious and they are focused on furthering their career. Some comedians are jealous. "Some comics have no use for you unless you are sleeping with them or writing them jokes."

In a town like LA, it's competitive because there aren't as many places to work. So, "You feel like you must be funnier than the next guy."

Sometimes there is hostility. People talk behind your back. "Sometimes, you feel entrenchment from people who have been here a long time and don't want to lose their place."

"When you first get into town, people check you out. It's almost like being strip-searched: What is his material? Is he a thief? Is his material original? Is it generic?"

There is "one-upsmanship" on stage and off. As one comic describes it, "If someone is killing, I think, 'I'm going to destroy this room.' If no one is laughing, I think, 'I know they want to laugh now, so I'm going to make it impossible for them not to laugh.'" In addition, offstage there is lots of playfully insulting one another to win status. "You learn to look for what there is to insult about someone."

However, comic Tom Ryan noted, "the competition can be good, if the comic thinks, "I can do as well as he/she is. Start working harder."[(64)]

> The headliner's set is the show's climax. The crescendo. The finale. You want the audience to walk away saying, "Oh, I want to see that headliner again!" You want the repeat business; therefore, you must stand out as being the best of the evening.
>
> Craig Shoemaker

CHAPTER 6

THE HEADLINER PHASE: 5 YEARS + MASTERS OF THEIR CRAFT

AUDIENCES CAN BE HEAVEN—AND HELL

Which One's the Dummy?

One night when I was MC'ing a show, one woman kept heckling the ventriloquist, David Strassman. Through his puppet, "Chuck," Strassman kept ripping this woman apart. So, she got angrier and angrier at the puppet. Finally, she jumped up on stage, and literally took a swing at "Chuck," the dummy. They had to throw the woman out of the club. The funny thing is that the next morning, she probably didn't even remember that she tried to beat the daylights out of a piece of wood.

- Michael Pace

You Paid a Cover Charge to See a Show—So Why Are You Talking?

Comedian Kip Adotta was on stage one evening when his attention was drawn to a patron who was talking loudly. Kip went over to the side of the stage and said to the man, "You must be in great need of attention, so I am going to give you more attention than you wanted. Right now, you have two choices: you can either keep quiet, or you can leave the showroom. Which will it be?" At this point, the audience—who had been laughing hilariously just moments before—fell dead silent. The man, too, was now silent. Kip said, "If you are going to be quiet, I want you to tell me that you are going to be quiet." The man lowered his head and managed to stammer, "I will be quiet." In reply, Kip Adotta simply said, "Thank you." Kip resumed his show right where he left off, and the audience immediately resumed laughing.

- Bob Fisher
Owner, The Ice House

Don't Mess with the Mob!

One time I was doing a show at a mob-owned club back East. There was a woman who was very drunk, and she threw an ashtray at me on stage. Fortunately for me, she was not a great shot, and the ashtray missed hitting me in the eye. Unfortunately for her, the ashtray hit a large neon backdrop behind me. I later learned that neon sign cost $20,000. A couple of burley "security guys" escorted the woman and her husband out of the show room, and I continued the show with the shattered sign hissing and crackling.

After the performance, I went backstage to collect my paycheck. I happened to see the woman and her husband in a room along with several very tough looking "gentlemen." The couple had obviously been beaten very badly and blood had been shed. All of the couple's jewelry was sitting on the table, and I learned that they had been made to empty their bank accounts. The club was determined to collect for the damage to the neon backdrop. When they saw me, the couple cursed me out and blamed me for what had happened. The woman was so angry, and she had irritated the "goodfellas" so much, that one of them asked me if I wanted to get in a "shot" at her. I declined, politely, and simply told the couple that what happened to them wasn't my fault: I didn't throw the ashtray. However, this story doesn't end there. The club stiffed me for $1,000, and they offered to pay me in cocaine.

- Anonymous

CHAPTER 6

THE HEADLINER PHASE: 5 YEARS + "MASTERS OF THEIR CRAFT"

As a headliner, it's your job to "rock the house"—
and to bring it home for the club.
Ant

Overview of the Headliner Phase

The Headliner phase is characterized by the mastery of one's craft and the acquisition of "confidence that shows" in one's writing, performing, and audience management skills. The headliner is the "main attraction," and, as the final act, he or she shoulders the responsibility for the show.

It is as a headliner that the comic reaches the fullest understanding of the business, assumes the greatest responsibility, and receives the most rewards. As comedian Rudy Moreno describes it:

> Headlining is the end result of all your hard work. You can really have fun with the audience. As a headliner, you not only get more respect from other comics, but from the audience and club owners.[43]

Headlining is also the final, dues-paying preparation for television and films. And, for a select few who are very good and very lucky, headlining is the path to "superstardom."

<u>What Happens During the Headliner Stage</u>

The significant experiences that occur during the headlining stage are:

- Making the shift from middle act to headlining
- Learning the responsibilities of headlining
- Navigating growth and challenges in the headliner's writing
- Changes in one's comic persona as a headliner
- Growth in one's performing skills as a headliner
- Changes in one's audience skills as a headliner
- Enjoying the best things about headlining
- Learning to manage the worst things about headlining
- Overcoming the biggest challenges of headlining
- Growth in one's skills in different performing venues
- Learning the business aspects of performing at the headlining stage
- Paying your dues and making a living at headliner
- Superstardom: a desired outcome of the headliner phase

Making the Shift from Middle Act to Headlining

The comics report that moving from middle to headliner can involve an introspective assessment of one's readiness. As Michael Jr. recalls:

> When I was first asked to headline, I was happy to be asked, but I turned it down. I didn't feel like I was ready. I didn't have a strong show with a really big closer where people would remember me. It wasn't until a year later (at about the five-year mark) that I felt I was ready. I noticed that it was getting harder for the headliner to follow me.(49)

The shift from middle act to headlining can also involve "getting past the fear," as the comedian Ant illustrates:

> I was reluctant at first because I felt I wasn't good enough. When my management pushed me, I did it. It was the scariest week of my life, but I did it. It was then that I realized that I needed to have the same faith in myself that others did in me.(41)

Ant adds that, for him, the transition to headlining came down to several questions:

- Do you have a *strong* forty-five minutes to an hour of material?
- Do you have confidence in your ability *every* time you go onstage?
- Are you willing to grow?(41)

Ant recalls that he realized he was ready to headline after he had answered those questions "yes," and then tried it. He adds:

> I had the material, honed over nine years. I had the performing experience that only going up every night can give you. I knew the different types of crowds and how to work them. And, I had the support of my managers. That was a big one for me.[41]

Ant suggests that aspiring headliners also consider the following questions before headlining:

- Are you willing to drop your act if it isn't going well and talk to the crowd?

- Can you handle hecklers?

- Do you have a plan "B" if the set isn't going well?

- Can you change-up your act at a second's notice?

- Can you "hit a home run" on stage consistently?[41]

Comedian/producer Vic Dunlop agrees that in order to headline, the performer must be consistent:

> If you want to headline, you had better be able to put on a good show ninety-nine percent of the time. And, the other one percent had better be

> because you are sick—or because they, the audience, stinks.
>
> As a headliner, you are wearing the crown, and you've got two guys performing in front of you who want that crown. You had better be funnier than they are.[47]

Comic Jeff Garcia states that he would tell someone who was moving from middle to headlining, "Pace yourself, and be memorable." Garcia explains:

> Doing twenty minutes is like running a sprint; headlining is like running a mile. When you headline, if you come out too quickly you're going to run out of gas. You must pace yourself.
>
> Another thing I would tell a new headliner is to, "Say something memorable." Come up with something that gives people a way to remember you and that differentiates you from other comics. You're not going to make money if they go, "Who's the guy who does that?"[53]

Comic Kevin Jordan tells middlers who want to headline, "If you are a *true* headliner, have enough material to cover *anything* that happens." Jordan explains:

> The first time somebody said to me, "Can you close?" I said, "Yeah, sure." If I look back honestly, though, I shouldn't have been closing the

> show. I had maybe twenty-five minutes of material, which I had to stretch to forty-five. But, if you are going to be a real headliner, have the *true time.* You must be able to do a very solid forty-five minutes.[54]

Comic Rocky LaPorte agrees and adds:

> To headline you have to be able to go up for thirty minutes and pound them [Make them laugh]. Tape your set. Make sure there is no fat in there and no down time. Then, you need to have another half hour that is just as strong. If the crowd isn't with you, you will go through an hour of material in forty-five minutes. When the crowd is laughed out, and a lot of premises have been burned, you will need ample "A" material.[42]

Comic Kevin Jordan further observes that by the time you get to the headliner stage, "You should have your 'stuff' together from top to bottom." He explains:

> You should know how to dress on stage. If somebody says, "I need six minutes," you should know which six minutes you are going to do. If they say, "Do eight minutes instead of six" or "I need an hour"—be able to do that.
>
> Your tapes and your press package should look professional. No more writing your name on a tape; you should have labels. It's time to *be* a professional.[54]

> Also, unless you are doing a character, your material should reflect who you are as an individual. These are the things that separate the good headliners from the poor ones.[54]

Jordan also points out that as a headliner, "You must be able to deal with all distractions smoothly and effectively." He states:

> When you become a headliner, you must deal with distractions like checks going out, the second round of drinks coming out, and people getting up and going to the bathroom. You must learn to handle all those things—and still do a good, strong, show.[54]

Finally, Jordan observes that, "You know you can headline when there are no more curveballs and no more surprises." Jordan explains:

> I've been on stage when the lights have gone out and when the microphone has gone dead. I've been on stage when a guy has had a seizure right in front of me, and when there has been a heart attack in the crowd. As a headliner, you must be able to handle anything that comes up, very calmly and confidently.[54]

Learning the Meaning of R-e-s-p-o-n-s-i-b-i-l-i-t-y

As a headliner, the comic learns that *he* is responsible for the show. As comic Tom Ryan put it: "Now, *I'm* their night-out. As a middle act, I wasn't."

The headliner is the "draw," and it is his name on the marquee. In addition, because he is the final act, the headliner *must* be good. Comedian Darren Carter explains:

> As the headliner, there is more pressure to make it worthwhile for everybody. When I was in the middle, if I was better than the headliner, that was great; it was a bonus. But when people are expecting you to be better, you really do have to "bring it."(48)

Kevin Jordan adds that as a headliner, "It is considered your show, good or bad." Jordan explains:

> If it's a bad show, they only blame the headliner. If it's a good show, you get the accolades. People who come up after the show to congratulate you will sometimes even look right at the opening act, point at the headliner, and say, "Wasn't he [the headliner] funny?" It's kind of rude; but hey, it's your show!(54)

Often, there is added pressure and responsibility for the headliner to "close strong." For instance, as Steve McGrew put it, "There are times you can see, in advance, that your performance is not going to be an easy one." He explains:

> The headliner must do forty-five minutes, even though it might not be the best night or the best audience. As the last performer, you can watch the other two comics go up and struggle,

> and you think, "Okay—now it's my turn."

Comedian Paul Provenza observes that as a headliner, "You learn what the phrase 'the show must go on' means." Comic Tim Jones describes this work ethic as follows:

> At the most difficult moments, that's when you see who has achieved a level of professionalism and can give a good show, no matter what—and who hasn't achieved that yet. It takes years of experience to go on stage and do that.(12)

Comic Steve Altman provides the following example of this performing ethic. Altman was on stage in Chicago one night doing a Michael Jackson-style "moonwalk." He walked off the edge of the stage and fell into the corner of a table. Altman recalls:

> I thought I had punctured a lung. When I didn't cough-up blood, I continued the show. I thought, "The show must go on." I figured that if I were really hurt, I'd faint and they would take me to the hospital. After the show, I called my doctor. As it turned out, I had broken a rib.(51)

Kevin Jordan reports that, "Another type of pressure or responsibility you feel when you are a headliner is that you are expected to break through." Diane Nichols agrees and adds, "Other people, including your peers, track your career." Nichols explains:

> At the headline stage, the pressure is phenomenal. People ask, "Why haven't you done this or that?" And, nobody forgets. I was supposed to do the *Late Show* one time, and two or three people mentioned that I wasn't on. People watch every move you make. You lose some of the fun, and you're in bigger and bigger stakes.[4]

Finally, Jeff Garcia describes the responsibility and pressure that are on the headliner to "sell tickets." Garcia states:

> I'm more scared of headlining now than when I first started. I think it's because *I* sell tickets now. The crowd is paying to see me, specifically. They are coming to see if this fool is funny, and I'd better be funny. *As a headliner, you must sell tickets.* That isn't something you even think about when you are middling.[53]

<u>Growth and Challenges in the Headliner's Writing Skills</u>

Comedian Rudy Moreno states that as a headliner, growth in one's writing skills means, "You try to get a little more clever, and you come up with material that has broader appeal." Comic Rick Sandack adds that at headliner, the comic also works on "developing a more mature and more cohesive act." Sandack recalls:

> It took me six years to be able to develop meaningful segues from one piece to another so that my act

> sounds cohesive and where people can look at me and say, "I think I know who he is as a person."[6]
>
> It's also about revealing yourself more as a human being. At this level, it's not just "Look at me, aren't I funny? Look at me, aren't I the life of the party?" It's being a full adult, in control, and willing to share yourself. It's about having some understanding about yourself.[6]

Growth as a writer also involves developing confidence in your writing ability. Darren Carter describes the confidence that the headliner acquires this way:

> As a headliner, I'm able to talk about whatever pops into my mind. Also, if something funny happened during the day, I can talk about it and *make* it work, and I have the confidence that it *will* work. And, if it doesn't work, it doesn't matter. I just go on with my material.[48]

Carter further explains that this confidence in one's writing skills also has other benefits. He adds:

> Now, as a headliner, I won't say, "I suck. They hate me." The truth is that they don't hate you. That particular joke didn't work. So what? That is the kind of confidence that has come as a headliner.[49]

Comic Steve Altman reports that one of the challenges with writing at the headliner stage is for the comic to "keep writing." Altman states:

> When you hit headliner status, there is a tendency to coast. My biggest lesson was hanging around Jerry Seinfeld and Larry Miller in the mid 1980s in Houston. The other comics said, "Hey, we're going to see a movie. Want to come?" They would say, "No, thanks. We're going to stay here and write." All they cared about was writing. They were headliners, but that's *why* they were headliners. They would edit and edit to make the joke as short and concise as possible. They were really into the craft of the joke.[51]

Kathy Buckley agrees that some comics may not write enough new jokes once they become headliners. Buckley points out, "Sometimes you can get lazy. Sometimes you can get comfortable with what works. And, it's scary to try out new stuff." Comic Tom Ryan offers the following explanation of why it can be hard for the headliner to write:

> You get to worrying about other things. A lot of your mental energy goes into finding work. You get worried about not wanting to screw things up, and it's just so much easier *not* to put in the hard work.
>
> When you have twenty minutes of material, the drive is built in: You've

> got to get to thirty minutes, then forty-five. But then, after you headline for a while and do more TV, you learn that TV burns up a lot of material, so you go back to writing.[(64)]

Writing a new forty-five minutes of material has been described as the equivalent of writing a new novel. Faced with that prospect, several comics report that sometimes there is an active resistance to writing new material. Kevin Jordan illustrates:

> One headliner actually told me, "It is easier for me to find a new audience than it is for me to write a new act." Another comic told me, "Hey, Shakespeare don't change his plays."[(54)]

Changes in One's Comic Persona at Headliner

For some performers, the comic persona continues to evolve at the headline stage. As Ant explains:

> My persona has definitely become more well-defined on stage. I have a much clearer voice in my stand-up. Now, I really know what I want to say.[(41)]

Tom Ryan states that after nineteen years, he is still working on elements of his stage persona:

> People think I have my voice, but I'm not convinced I have found how I *should be* on stage. Some people find that earlier on; I'm still tinkering with

> it. Now, I'm trying to get a little more goofy; I'm still too inhibited on stage. I also have some good rant styles that I do, and I want to "bring my rage to the stage."[(64)]

Finally, several comics described going through a reassessment of their persona at about the ten-year point. Fritz Coleman called this a "mid-life crisis of being a comedian":

> It's almost as if you get to a point where you've mastered the craft and you know how to make people laugh, and you start thinking, "Now, what do I want to do as an artist? Am I going to be true to my comedic sense and creativity, or give the audience the 'dirty' material they want?"[(15)]
>
> You have to go through that, though. For Lenny Bruce to make the political statements he did, he had to know the structure of being a comedian and know the ebb and flow of crowd control. You have to know the basics before you can become an All-Star. *When the basics become second nature, only then can what is profound, brilliant, and unique emerge.*[(15)]

<u>Growth in One's Performing Skills at Headliner</u>

As a headliner, the comedian must learn how to structure his material for a performance that is forty-five minutes or longer. As Ant illustrates:

> My act is structured differently now. Now I have a strong open, strong middle, and a killer close. Before I had a strong open and killer close, because twenty minutes isn't that much time to really "wow" a crowd.[41]

The comic also learns increasingly sophisticated ways to *pace* his act as a headliner. Paul Provenza illustrates:

> At middle, I was refining rhythm and building crescendos. Then, when I started headlining, I couldn't do that anymore. With the extra fifteen minutes, if you keep building, people get exhausted. At middle, I used to tag and tag. Then, what I had to learn to do was to get the peaks and troughs. I had to learn how to get a nice lift and then a little relaxation, and then a nicer lift.[37]

At this stage, the comic also develops the ability to think ahead and choose material from his joke file *during* a performance. Jimmy Burns describes this skill as "flipping through a card file in your head." Another comedienne observes, "It's like you have this computer menu in your head, and you make the menu real small at the top right corner of your brain. And, as you are doing your act, you just keep looking up at the menu."[20] She adds:

> Some, but not all, comics work two to three bits ahead. I don't. I work about a half a bit ahead. I'll be half way

> through something and then I will decide what to move on to.[20]

Michael Jr. observes "That's the key to headlining, when you can think about what to do on the fly, instead of having a set that's strictly pre-determined." He states:

> While I am performing, I'm thinking about the third joke down the line and how it might flow with the reaction of the people to the current joke.[49]

Tom Ryan adds, "Sometimes when you are mentally editing several bits ahead to get a smoother segue, you even forget that you have just delivered a punch line!"

Steve McGrew states that one of the performing skills he developed as a headliner was to "read his audiences." McGrew explains:

> As a headliner, you must learn to evaluate your audience. I always try to read my audience. Are they couples? Are they singles? Are they a minority group?[44]

Mc Grew adds:

> I've worked very hard to figure out what works with audiences and what doesn't. I've never figured out why guys do material that they aren't pretty certain is going to work with an audience.[44]

Ant agrees that evaluating audiences can help the comic avoid failure, and he describes another technique that a headliner learns to create variety in his performance. Ant states:

> I am much more attuned to my crowds now. For example, if I do a joke about sex and it doesn't do well, I know to move away from that topic and go on to something else.
>
> Also, I have many more "act outs" now (bits that I act out) in my set. I found that audiences really responded better to those rather than my presenting only jokes with a set-up and punch line.[41]

Eddie Merrill describes the performing flexibility a headliner develops this way:

> You'll have pieces that go anywhere from thirty seconds to six minutes on one single topic. That way, I can plug them in whenever I want to, and none of my shows are exactly the same. Some routines can go for six minutes or I can cut four or five jokes and do four minutes. It depends on how the audience reacts, how much time I have to perform, and what I want to do.[21]

As headliners, the comics also master the use of the space on stage. Darren Carter explains:

> I did a show in Houston and got to do "Theatre in the Round" where the stage is a circle and there are people all around you. That stuff didn't happen when I was an opener or a middle act. As a headliner, I have also learned to work every square inch of the stage.[48]

In addition, because it is a live performance, a headliner learns to take advantage of whatever is going on in the room during his show. As comic Steve Altman describes it, "You learn that everything is fodder.":

> Everything that is going on has comic potential. You're in a live situation. If someone drops a glass, you use it. You address a funny shirt or a funny laugh. That injects intimacy into a performance. It tailors a performance, and it keeps your performances from being "the same old thing."[51]

To enhance his performance, the headliner also relies on his instinct and experience to better evaluate questions such as: "Is this cute?" "Is it worthwhile for me to deal with this?" and, "Is it funnier than what I was going to do?"[12]

Darren Carter adds, "As a headliner, you learn how to perform for the crowd that's in front of you." Carter explains:

> Don't just recite well-written material. There has to be a level of entertaining that particular crowd. You might want to break away from your act and talk to them. Or, if you don't want to talk to them, don't just go down your set list from A to Z. Start out with A, but then you move on to J and then back to F.[48]

Kevin Jordan agrees that personalizing one's performance is important:

> Anytime you can make a show more personal it's better. If you are doing a show for a special group, I feel that the show should reflect the group.
>
> For example, when I do a corporate show, I study up on the company's background. If I'm doing a show for the military, I will do military material. I do my homework as to what they like, what they know, and what the people in the group might talk about.[54]

Kevin Jordan states that as a headliner you learn that, no matter how large the crowd is or how small the venue, you must bring your full energy to your performance. Jordan explains:

> Whether the show is for 10, 50, 500, or 5,000 people, you have to bring the energy. Ten people paid to see a show the same as 1,000 did. If you are

> acting in a play, you don't say, "Oh, it isn't a packed house so who cares." If you are a professional entertainer, don't just go through the motions. Audiences will notice it if you do. Owners will notice it, and you'll know it.[54]

Growth in One's Audience Skills at Headliner

At the headline stage, the comics state that they developed a greater enjoyment and appreciation of audiences. Ant provides the following illustration:

> Now, the audience is my favorite part of the experience. I love talking to crowds. That wasn't always the case. I never trusted my natural wit, so I never engaged them. Now, with the confidence I have, I really do enjoy making my show more interactive. I also enjoy "calling back" things I have learned from the audience and then incorporating those things into some of my established bits.[41]

Kathy Buckley states that, "As a headliner, I've become one with my audience when I perform." Buckley adds:

> The audience is my family for that time being. When I hit the stage, I think, "Okay, I'm here. I'm going to take your problems away for a little while. You sit back and relax. We're going to have some fun."[63]

In the following excerpt, Michael Jr. illustrates the sophisticated ways in which a headliner will come to *use the audience as a writing partner*:

> As a headliner, my writing skills have gotten stronger. But, the audience will always be funnier than you; I mean that *their imagination* is. You begin to say something and give them a look, and they will fill in the punch line stronger than you ever could. It's really a matter of getting them to use their imagination.
>
> If you draw a picture *for* them, they'll understand it. But, if you can make *them* draw a picture that you want them to see, with their own personal touch on it, *it gives each of them a reason to laugh*. If you give them too much, it turns into your picture instead of their own. It's a fine line.[49]

Comic Eddie Merrill compares this process to "an artist drawing on a pallet." Merrill states:

> I do a joke that consistently gets a groan from the audience. I think, "Yes, it's a sad concept, but I'm just a big guy talking to you. I've painted something in your mind that you don't like. It's not me you don't like; it's the picture that you painted in your mind."

> The fact that the majority of the audience can laugh at it means that I have done a good job of painting.(21)

Merrill adds:

> I set the mood and the audience responds to it. If you look at a painting, you're going to get a different feeling than the person next to you, and you may get a different feeling than the artist intended.(21)

By the time he headlines, the comic has typically found *his* audience. He has discovered the crowds who seem to like his material and/or persona—and those who don't. However, as Tom Ryan observes, at the headliner stage the comic is faced with *finding his audience on a broader basis*, for example, through radio, the Internet, television, concert venues, or through the corporate circuit.

Handling Hecklers as a Headliner

Comic Darren Carter describes the performing confidence that one acquires as a headliner—and how that impacts the way the comic handles hecklers at this stage:

> If somebody yells out something, I am now able to bring my style to it and just play with them. Most of the time they are not there to hurt the show; they are just there to have fun. As an opening or middle act, I was not as confident. My first instinct was to make them shut up. I would say something to quickly put them in their place.

> Now, that's not my style. But, it's kind of like judo. You take their most aggressive move, and then use it against them.[48]

Jeff Garcia offers the following advice for the newer headliner when it comes to dealing with disruptive audience members:

> The new headliner wants to get mad at an interruption, when the best way to shut them down is to be nice to the person. You can't lose your cool. You have to be the calmest you can be in order to take care of your job. Sometimes, you just have to step back a little bit and just stay cool.[53]

Some headliners, like Rocky LaPorte, will even use an index finger to their lips (a gentle "be quiet" motion) after an initial heckle to silence someone rather than immediately insulting the audience member. LaPorte states:

> I don't like to attack at all. Attacking is not really in keeping with my character. I try to be nice. I don't want to ruin the show. For me, a gentle signal to be quiet works.[42]

LaPorte adds:

> Sometimes the audience reminds me of school kids: you have to go up there and settle them down. Sometimes they are like babies: you have

> to soothe them. The only thing that ruins that is when they have too much to drink. Then, that's when you call for club security. You can't allow 300 people to have a bad time because of a couple of drunks.(42)

Like Rocky LaPorte, some comics feel that "being nice first" shows respect to the audience. As one comic phrased it, "It gives the talker or heckler a chance to conform, and it gives the comic time to assess the heckler's intent."(39) It also shows that the comic is confident and in control of him or herself even when the audience member was rude.

On the other hand, as comic Tom Ryan describes it, "Even at the headliner stage, sometimes it's a crap shoot with audiences." Ryan explains:

> Every now and then your number comes up, and you'll get an audience that just doesn't like you—*and* they'll get hostile about it. It is more or less them saying, "We disagree with what you think is funny." The comic is saying, "I think this is funny." They're saying, "No, you're wrong." So, there is a battle of the wills that goes on, and sometimes it can get hostile.(64)

<u>Growth in Improvising with Audiences</u>

Some comics come to love improvising with audiences at this stage. Steve Altman provides such an example:

> Now, I love talking to people. I've gone twenty minutes not doing material. It keeps things fresh. I was scared to death of that early on. But, that "improv" muscle is so important. If you are not afraid to let go and be in the moment, then improvising is the best.[51]

Altman adds:

> Improvising gives you the confidence that you *can* go off-script and be good. If you let yourself be "in the moment," *you'll be funny*. You *are* funny. You wouldn't be on stage if you *weren't* funny. So, have the confidence that whatever comes out of your mouth, in the moment, will be funny.[51]

Native American comedian Charlie Hill reports that improvising with audiences also has other rewards, such as a feeling of pride in one's creativity. Hill states:

> Sometimes, when you are up there and you start improvising, and it goes well, it's like *soaring* out there. It's like kissing God, because I believe God has a hand in that creativity.[33]

Kevin Jordan reports that interacting with audiences can be useful for the comic because, "sometimes, people in the audience will say things that you just can't make up." However, Jordan also acknowledges, "Even at headliner, some guys don't interact with the audience." Jordan explains:

> For some guys, their act is way it is going to be. Period. It's purely scripted. I don't say it's bad, but that's just what they do.[54]

Comic Billy Gardell provides one example of why some veterans don't improvise with audiences. Gardell states:

> I don't want to talk to audiences. They didn't pay their money for me to talk to them. I feel that they came to see a show.[65]

Growth in One's Skills with Different Performing Venues

A headliner's growth with respect to performing venues often means gleaning information about a new performing venue prior to a performance. Comic Joey Gaynor reports that this process can even begin on the way to the club. Gaynor states:

> Do your homework. Look around you. Learn some local things about the club you are playing so that you can incorporate those things into your act. If you have a joke about a drug store, mention the large one you saw down the street. If you have jokes about a used car lot or about a cheap motel, refer to the one you saw on the way into town.[52]

Comic/producer Steve Bluestein agrees and adds:

> I always check out the city. I check out what the biggest local supermarket is and what the local attractions are. In the car on the way in from the airport, I'll have ten questions for the driver.[57]

Mastering the art of working in different venues also involves respecting the club you are visiting. Kathy Buckley, for instance, offers the following advice:

> Be nice to people wherever you are working. This is their home, their workplace. This is their livelihood. The club is not a place to have an ego. It's not a place to make a lot of demands. You're a comic. If you've got a microphone, you're all set. You're a guest in somebody's club. Being disrespectful is unnecessary.[63]

Steve Altman adds that being courteous to the staff of the clubs you visit not only shows good manners, it's also "good business." Altman explains:

> Get to know the sound guys, the lighting, the wait staff, and the management. It adds to the vibe. I hear about so many comics who say, "Oh, that guy is such a jerk." And, every time that comic comes back to the club, there is going to be negative energy. You want to nurture positive energy,

> especially in a comedy club. You also want to get the staff saying, "Hey, you've got to see this guy." Someone may be a good comic, but he only hurts himself if the staff says, "I'm not going to tell anybody he's here."[51]

Comedian Ant observes that *showing respect for different crowds* is important as you travel. Ant notes, for example:

> If you are working a clean room, respect that and don't curse. Understand the area where you are performing. If you are working the Bible Belt, don't insult them.[41]

Comic Joey Gaynor agrees and adds:

> Respect the fact that in "red" states, certain material may not go over. You might make enemies you don't want to make. If an audience doesn't laugh, move on to something else. You are there to entertain, and you don't want to look unfunny.[52]

As a middle act or headliner, the comic learns more about the qualities of different venues that can affect a performance. For example, Tom Ryan notes that even the *temperature of a room* can be a major factor in the success of a show. Ryan explains:

> It's a comedic fact that if it's hot in the room, people don't laugh. They are busy fanning themselves and they're

> distracted. I do a lot of corporate gigs now. When I go in, I say, "You've paid a lot of money. Make one little adjustment to the temperature, [cool the room] and the show will go a lot better."(64)

According to several comics, comedy also works better in venues with low ceilings. Tom Ryan explains:

> With low ceilings, there is more intimacy and there is less room for the eyes to wander. Low ceilings almost force the audience to focus on the stage, and the laughter is more contained, sound-wise.(64)

Several comics report that a smart headliner will take the time to evaluate a new performing venue. Larry Omaha, for instance, recalls:

> I learned to go in and check out every place I was going to perform. I checked out where I entered from and how many steps I would have to go up. I wanted to know where I was supposed to stand ahead of time.(62)

Tim Jones agrees, and reports that he will go into a new show room in the afternoon when nobody is there to check it out. Jones explains:

> I'll sit on the stage and get a sense of the room. Then, I'll sit in different

> parts of the room so I can see what they see. If somebody is heckling me, I want to see what they are seeing. I want to see what the stage is like from this angle and that. I want to see if they're seated at comfortable tables or if they are jammed in.
>
> Then, in the early evening when the staff starts coming in, you just sense their energy. If the club owner is a loose kind of club manager, it's a relaxed atmosphere. There are other owners who have 1,000 rules. You can sense the tension.
>
> Checking out a new room helps me, because that way I'm not walking in to a new place "cold."[12]

Jones adds that he also likes to observe a new room on opening night. He states:

> Checking the room also shapes how I do my show. For instance, I saw that one room had a dance floor. There was a stage, the dance floor, and then the audience. They had put some chairs on the dance floor, but it was like a pit. If I talked to somebody down there, nobody could see the person sitting in the pit.
>
> The first two comics didn't realize that, and they talked to the people

> down there. By sitting in the back of the room earlier, I saw, "Don't spend time down there, because you are going to lose the rest of the room."[(12)]

Finally, Steve Altman describes an additional benefit that a comic gains from surveying a larger venue. Altman recalls:

> There was this gigantic place in Hemet, California. I was watching the first guy, and I heard an echo, so I started walking around to listen to the sound system. And, I thought, "This guy is talking too fast." I turned to the second act, and said, "Hey man, they can't hear because of the echo going back and forth. The laughter happens, and it happens in waves." He said, "Okay." So, he went on and he slowed it down a bit, and it still sounded too fast to me. So, I got up there and really started talking slowly, and it worked.[(51)]

<u>Learning the Business Aspects of Performing as a Headliner</u>

As a headliner, the comic must learn many new things about the business side of comedy. Comic Darren Carter illustrates the kinds of things that a young headliner might learn about the business. He states:

- Have posters and cards made up so people know that you are coming to town. That way, more people show up. You also develop a following that way. The more you develop a following, the more you get a percentage of the door; and that motivates everybody.

- Do a tour of different radio stations during the week that you're in a town.
- Sell your CDs, DVDs, and T-shirts after your performances, and sign them.
- Keep in contact with your fans through your Website. Maintain an email list so that people will get an email when you are going to be in their town.
- When you do a radio spot, bring your CD so the DJ can play some two-minute segments.(48)

As the comic's career progresses, other people such as personal managers enter the picture and begin to help the comic with business issues and career decisions. As the comedian becomes a more marketable commodity, more money is involved and decisions multiply exponentially.

A good manager can be very important in directing a career. Theatrical agents, comedy agents, booking agents, and TV or radio commercial agents can help the comic make connections to jobs. A good agent will get the comic interviews and he keeps the comic's name circulating. Jeff Garcia notes that good management also can help the comic manage money issues:

> My manager didn't find the part in the Jimmy Neutron movie for me, but when it came up, they called him and he took care of the numbers. Agents

> will also "smack" the club people for money. That's their job. I don't go in there and argue.
>
> Also, a club might say, "Come and work for this amount," and I might be fine with it. But, my agent got me *a lot* more. Also, on my own, I might lag behind; for instance, the headshots might not go out or I'll use old headshots. That sort of thing is going to hurt your business.[53]

Ant adds that it is important for the headliner to make sure he or she has good people around him. He points out:

> Good management can get you into more "A" rooms, increase your television exposure, make you a brand name, and move you into the next level. That means getting a development deal with a network.[41]

However, as one comic notes, not all agents/managers are trustworthy or good at their jobs.[39] Some agents do not work hard at securing jobs for the performer and don't send the comic out on enough interviews. Others handle too many clients of the comic's "type," or do not have access to the latest information. Some agents make bad deals, book bad jobs, or push the comic aside to promote favored clients. In the worst cases, a bad agent may cheat or sabotage the comic. Eddie Merrill cautions that, "Some agents may be hungrier than others, and some might understand the business better."[21]

For these reasons, the comics indicated that the performer should be actively involved in planning his career and he must be aware of all business decisions that are made on his behalf.

Comics also learned other ins-and-outs of the business: For example, Jeff Garcia reports that it's often smart business to be paid in cash or to be paid in advance:

> If the club hasn't been around for years, do *not* take a check. I've had guys give me pinkie rings and personal checks. And, if you hear anything suspicious about the promoter, tell them that you want your money up front.[(53)]

Kevin Jordan states that as a headliner you learn that it is a good business practice to "keep expanding your circle of work." Jordan explains:

> I tell beginners that when you MC or open, there is a lot of work. There is still a lot of work for feature acts. However, when you move up to headliner, there are 1,000 headliners and only fifty-two weeks. There is less room at the top, and you find work harder to get. So, I tell comics, "Every year you should widen your circle of work. If you worked ten clubs last year, strive to work fifteen this year because you are going to lose a few clubs."[(54)]

Finally, learning about different aspects of the business can also help the comic move into producing, writing, selling a pilot, etc., should they decide to leave performing or choose to explore new business ventures.[2]

<u>The Best Things about Headlining</u>

When asked, "What are the best things about headlining?" the comics describe a wide variety of benefits. For example, comic Charlie Hill observes that:

> The best thing about headlining is that you are the writer, director, and star. When it goes well, it's all *you*, and that is the best feeling in the world.[33]

Ant summarizes some of the benefits of headlining this way:

> The money is *a lot* better! The prestige of headlining is great. And, the ability to move upward to working in better rooms is great, because there really are "A" rooms and "B" rooms.[41]

Comedian John Fox describes the "benefits" of being a headliner in the following humorous terms:

> I have the greatest job in the world. I work for one hour a day. I drink on the job. The boss buys me drinks. I get to travel all over the world. That's a pretty good gig. I looked in the paper, and you just can't find other jobs like that. My only problem, is that I keep getting older—and the cocktail waitresses don't![56]

Another benefit of being a headliner is the confidence that comes with knowing that *you* are "the draw." Comic Steve McGrew explains:

> As the headliner, people are coming to see *you*. You don't have to feel like, "Oh, I *hope* the audience likes me; I know that they are really here to see the headliner." To me, that's the best.[44]

Darren Carter adds that one of the perks of being a headliner is that "Sometimes, you get the celebrity treatment." Carter explains:

> As the headliner, you are the star that week. Often, you get to be on local radio stations in the morning and do their local television.[48]

Jeff Garcia agrees that headliners are treated better. He states:

> You get the best room when you go out of town. If they are opening a new restaurant, the headliner might be invited to the opening.[53]

Another benefit of headlining (and working in show business) is the opportunity to meet other celebrities. Rocky LaPorte provides the following illustration:

> I've gotten to meet some really cool people like the Rolling Stones, the Beach Boys, and the Temptations. I'm

> a fan, and I really get a kick out of that.[42]

Michael Jr. points out, "One of the best things about headlining is that you get all that time on stage with people."[49] Ant agrees and states, "I was always a performer. Now, as a headliner, *people have forty-five minutes to really see my performing skills.*"[41] Darren Carter adds that, "As a headliner, I'm able to do *a greater variety of things to entertain audiences* when I perform." Carter states:

> I'm not just one topic or one style. I become characters. I do impressions, one-liners, and stories. If you are performing for a shorter time, it's harder to do all of those things. *With a shorter set, it's harder to showcase your versatility.*[48]

Larry Omaha reports that headlining also has the benefit of being creatively satisfying "because it allows you to stretch as a performer." Omaha explains:

> A headline set over several days represents a chance to become sharper, add nuances and innuendos, and hone your timing. You don't have that opportunity in the fifteen-to twenty-minute sets at the showcase clubs.[62]

As a headliner, having more time to establish who you are as a performer also has other benefits, as Steve Altman explains:

> When the audience gets to know you, you can do material that probably would not go over if you were doing an opening set. Sometimes they need to know who you are before they are able to "buy" a bit. Even material that isn't as strong may work once the audience gets to know you.[51]

Another benefit of headlining cited by the comics is the "power" that stand-up comedy affords the performer. Tim Jones provides the following example:

> Comedy is real power. Comedy is basically saying, "Laugh when I say laugh." Sometimes, you get a crowd that appreciates you and you love them, man. When comedy kicks in, there is nothing better. Maybe sex. There is no higher high. And, when you're bombing, there is no lower low.[12]

Diane Nichols agrees, and she describes another type of "power" that the comic has:

> With comedy, it's all up to you. You decide what to say. You get to voice your opinion, and you can even do things like sneak in your political beliefs.[4]

Nichols adds that:

> One downside of show business is that you always have to think about

> yourself and be self-evaluating. But, it's exhausting. Sometimes in bed, I'm thinking, "What is that noise? Is it my pulse? No, it's my throbbing ego!" I have to think of something else besides myself so I can calm down and get some sleep.[4]

Comic Charlie Hill speaks for many comics when he states that one benefit of a good headline set is that it can spark creativity. Hill explains:

> When I go to bed after a great set and I can't sleep, I'll even try to recreate that set in my mind. And, when I'm on the road, I will write after a great show.[33]

Another advantage of headlining is choosing *where you will work*. John Fox explains:

> After many years in the business, you can pick and choose from among better clubs. A lot of comics sleep in their cars and drive from gig to gig—to do "one-nighters" [in the back of a restaurant].[56]

Tim Jones adds that as a headliner you can often determine *with whom you will work*:

> As a headliner, you often get a say in what mix will work well with the show that you do. If a comic is too dirty or if you don't get along, you may not

> want to work with them. A lot of low-key headliners won't work with a high energy middle. It's in their contract. I was middling one time for someone whom I was blowing off stage. The headliner complained, and the owner cut my time to ten minutes.[12]

A headliner also derives benefits from having a fan base. Darren Carter illustrates.

> By the time you're headlining, you've also picked up a following because you've been on television. Some people will see you and say, "I've been watching you since I was a teenager." It makes you feel good because it's like, "Wow, this person knows me, and they like what I do."[48]

Carter further observes that, "If even a segment of the audience knows you, it can provide a significant boost to the show." Supportive audiences also trigger a *critical shift for the headliner's confidence*. Carter explains:

> You go from "Hey, I'm trying to make you laugh" to "Hey, this is funny; either you're with me or you're not. I *know* this stuff is funny, and I'm going to have a good time." That's such a better approach to performing than, "Gee, I hope you guys like me. Is this funny?"[48]

Another benefit of developing a fan base as a headliner is when audience members request certain material. Darren Carter describes the gratification a comic feels when an audience knows his work:

> People will have favorite bits that they will request and that's nice. You think, "Oh, cool. They know that bit."[48]

Comic Rocky LaPorte reports that, "Getting a standing ovation is one of the best perks of the job." LaPorte explains:

> Just to know that you have affected so many people so positively is great. There is a lot of love going on in a room when everybody is laughing. You are not thinking about your bills, or your troubles, or that your back is hurting. You are free in that moment. You and the audience are in sync, and everything is working and clicking. That's the best feeling in the world to me.[42]

Tom Ryan agrees and adds:

> There is no greater thrill than really killing in a packed house. When you connect with a crowd and have them in the palm of your hand, and you blow the roof off, there is nothing more exhilarating. When you are the final comic they saw that night, and they had a great night out, and you can tell, that's the best![64]

Finally, there are those audience moments that are extremely touching and profoundly gratifying for the comic. Such memorable audience encounters literally make the comedian's job worthwhile. Comic Kenny Kane, who entertained military troops in the Middle East, remembers one soldier who thanked him profusely after one show. Kane recalls:

> This guy couldn't thank me enough and I was almost embarrassed. Then, the soldier said, "You don't understand. I've got to go on a mission in a very dangerous area tomorrow morning, and I may not come back."

Vic Dunlop provides another example of a very poignant encounter with an audience member:

> After a show one time, a woman came up to me. She told me that exactly one year ago she and her husband had come to see my show. On the drive home they were in a terrible car accident and her husband was killed. She had had a very difficult year, and when she saw that I was in town, she said she knew she had to come to see my show. The woman hugged me, thanked me, and told me that she and her husband had had a wonderful time their last night together. She also told me that the show I had just finished was the first time she had laughed since the accident.[47]

The Worst Things about Headlining

Almost unanimously, the comics state that one of the worst things about headlining is the process of checks going out to the audience. Right in the middle of the headliner's show, the club patrons receive their bills, and many of them start discussing, debating, and reconciling their food and beverage tabs out loud. As one comic describes it, "When the checks go out, they won't even know you are up there." Comedian Ant describes his response to checks going out this way:

> That's when I stop my act and start talking to the crowd. Then, after I re-focus them, I continue with my act.[41]

Some comics find the check drop to be frustrating. Kathy Buckley, for example, states that, "Within fifteen minutes of getting on stage, you start hearing conversations like, "You owe twenty-four dollars," and "Who ordered X?" Sometimes, you just want to say, "Will you just split the bill already!" Comic Joey Gaynor voiced his irritation this way:

> What is the problem, people? You ate. You drank. Did you think you weren't going to have to pay? Why turn this into such a big production during my performance?[52]

Darren Carter reports that many headliners come up with creative ways to deal with the inevitable fact of the bills being handed out. He explains:

> Some comics stop and "call the moment." I will make a joke out of it. I'll

> say, "Oh, the servers are like comedy Grinches: they are passing out the bad news now." Some comics talk to the audience. Sometimes, I will do bits that are a little louder and more visual, so that it's a little more entertaining. That way, I can talk over people and make people tap their friend on the shoulder and say, "Quiet, I want to hear what he is saying." Other times, I try to "kill" really hard there so that nobody notices there is a distraction.[48]

Steve Altman adds that a number of comics will throw in a musical interlude at this point:

> A lot of musical guys will have a song for just this purpose. They will see the checks going out, and they'll say, "I'm going to do a song for you now." This is a good way to keep the show going while the audience members are paying their bills, and yet the performer is still entertaining them.[51]

On the other hand, several comics report that they do *not* address the fact that checks are going out. Steve McGrew, for example, states

> I just keep going. I might slow the show down a bit because I don't want to use my best stuff and have it not work. But, I never say, "Oh, great; the checks are going out. What did

> you have to drink?" I don't do that because some people just hand their credit card to the server and they keep watching the show.[44]

Larry Omaha agrees and adds that he doesn't mind checks going out. Omaha explains, "I want to be paid; therefore, they've got to pay their bills."

Another difficult aspect of doing stand-up is having their performance interrupted by audience members. Rocky LaPorte states, "For some reason, people think it's perfectly okay to yell things out during a live performance at a comedy club." LaPorte adds:

> When you write an act like mine that depends a lot on timing, if somebody yells something out, it blows the set-up or the punch line. I look at this as an art form or a performance, and they are *not* helping me *at all* when they do that. Some comics want that or they don't mind that. Those comics will go after the heckler and tear them up. But, that's not my style.[42]

The comics report that the first show on a Friday is often difficult because people have worked all day, rushed home, and then hurried to the show. They are tired, and by the time the headliner goes on, they are ready for bed. The comics also state that the *second show on Friday is the most difficult show all week.*[12] Tom Ryan explains:

> Sometimes there is a cool rowdiness that enhances the late show Friday.

> But, most of the time you are just waiting for the wheel to come off and unravel the whole show.[64]

Paul Provenza agrees, and adds:

> Boy, you could blindfold me, put me in a helicopter, and drop me on a stage anywhere in the country, and I can tell you if it is a Friday late show. People have been working all week, and it's a psychological relaxation thing. By the time I go on, they've had their two-drink minimum. So, they're tired *and* they've got alcohol in them. They are either extremely rowdy, or they're real tired. Even if they're with you at the beginning of your set, you can bank on it that by the end, you're not going to close as strongly because they are beat.[37]

Steve Altman and Gilbert Esquivel report that after performing two shows, the comic is also tired. Esquivel adds, "On a three-show night, I may start thinking, "Hey, have I done that joke already this set? Or was that during the second show?"[51, 85] Paul Provenza agrees and adds:

> I've actually seen veteran comics do the same joke during the same show, by mistake, on nights with three shows. That happens to people who have been doing it for years.[37]

Another difficult part of headlining is the occasional bad gig. John Wing explains:

> You don't know hell until you have played a university gig, it's "All the beer you can drink for $5 night," and you have to go on last. There is no hell like it. They don't want to listen. They're not into it. Although when they are not drunk, *students are the best-listening* audiences.[28]

Eddie Merrill describes some of the difficult bookings a comic may encounter this way:

> There is a broad range of experiences out there. For example, you might drive 300 miles to a job and hear: "Oh, you need a microphone? A stage? What, are you nuts? That costs money! Lighting? Here's a flashlight; they'll see you okay." Or, the joint can be a real toilet—and that's one of the better places. There are some bad, bad, bad places.[21]

Jeff Garcia describes the difficulty a headliner can have when he is booked to perform on holidays or dates that are undesirable for other reasons:

> Getting booked for really bad weeks is hard, like the Fourth of July weekend when people go out of town. Also, it's hard if they book me on a weekend some place where I would

> normally draw well and they are having a street fair with free beer near the club. There is no way to compete with that.
>
> Another time I went to Sacramento (which I can normally sell out), but they'd had Pablo Francisco and Carlos Mencia in the weeks immediately before me. We draw the same crowd. So, not being able to select your weeks can definitely be very frustrating.[53]

Bombing can still be a painful experience for headliners. As Tom Ryan described it:

> One of the worst things about headlining is when things turn south on you. You think, "I was their night out, and they had a lousy time." I feel bad. I did the best I could, and we just didn't connect. After a while, though, you realize, it's not life and death. Nobody got hurt.[64]

For some comics, however, the bad feeling lingers after a bad set. Charlie Hill explains:

> When you bomb, it's the worst feeling in the world. You can go home and tell your spouse, and they may sympathize, but they still don't know the feeling. Nobody knows but another comic. And, for me, that feeling

> lingers. It doesn't go away until the next time I'm on on stage and I get my first laugh.[33]

On the other hand, as one comic describes it, "There is nothing is funnier than watching your buddy bomb." Charlie Hill explains:

> The other comics will go, "Hey, hey, come watch; so and so is bombing." It's like animals. When one animal is dying, the others circle around so they can eat him. That's what it feels like, anyway. When you do well on the *Tonight Show*, people will say, "Great set." If you don't do well, comics will say, "What did you think of your last appearance?"[33]

The comics also spoke of another difficulty related to the business: rejection. Comedy is a tough business, and as comic Rocky LaPorte observes, "There are no guarantees of superstardom—even for headliners." LaPorte explains:

> This isn't the kind of job where if you put in twenty years they give you a gold watch. They don't automatically give you a TV sit-com or movie after X number of years. A lot of guys are bitter because they have not made it to the next level (superstardom). I tell them, "You had better like doing comedy, because you might just be working clubs and that's all. That's the risk we all take." Show business,

> in general, is mostly rejection. You get told "No"—a lot.[42]

Finally, as Jimmy Burns reports, leaving so much love from the audience when he finishes his set can be very difficult for the comic:

> [When you do really well] it's a magic moment. You just don't want to leave. You don't want to say "Goodbye." It's like a good sexual experience—you want to make it last as long as possible. In fact, it's the addictive part of performing. If I ever gave up comedy, I would have to stay away from the clubs.[39]

<u>The Biggest Challenges at the Headliner Stage</u>

One of the major challenges for the comic at this stage is the strain on their personal relationships. As comic Alonzo Bodden put it, "It's hard to tell a woman you're never going to be there on Saturday nights to take her out." Rocky LaPorte adds:

> It's hard to have relationships when you're on the road so much. I know a lot of guys and women whose marriages have busted up. You also don't get to see your kids too much. You're with someone, and then it's like, "I'll see you in two months." You're in a different bed every night. It wears on you. Plus your significant other gets insecure, and wants

> to know what you are doing. It's tough.[42]

Booking errors represent another challenge for the headliner. Vic Dunlop describes an unfortunate booking experience with one non-English speaking crowd:

> One time I did a corporate Christmas party in Los Angeles. The guy who booked me said, "Do thirty minutes. Keep it clean. It pays $1,500 for a weekday at lunchtime." I said, "Okay. I'm there." So, that day, I got on stage and started to do my act, and I didn't get one laugh. I looked around and noticed that they were all Japanese. None of them spoke English. I did my eyeball bit, and that got a few laughs. But, to stand there and have to do thirty minutes for an audience that doesn't speak your language was horrible. I did my time because I wasn't going to give the money back. But, I had a few choice words with the booker afterward.[47]

Another challenge facing headliners is that after they've worked their way up to headliner, they will frequently begin to go out on the road as an opening act for a major star. Tim Jones explains:

> It's kind of a vicious circle, except that you are making more money and staying in nicer places. But, you're back to "opener" again and

> you have to work your way back up to "star."[12]

Fritz Coleman agrees, and adds:

> Working as an opening act for a major star can be very good or very bad. If you do well, it's a "you've won them over" victory for you.
>
> Opening for a star or a band can also be a very bad experience. Often, the crowd is all excited before the big star gets there, and they are angry that you are the only thing that stands between them and the star they are paying big bucks to see. So, being an opening act at a concert can be very strange. I know some people who will never do it again.[15]

On the other hand, some comics argue that opening for a star represents an opportunity to learn. As Billy Gardell points out:

> You get to see what it's like at the next level. And, hopefully you take the good traits from the stars you open for and you apply them to your own career.[65]

Still another challenge for headliners can involve limiting their use of topical humor (i.e., current events). Steve Altman explains:

> When you are headlining, a lot of topical humor may have been done by the MC, the opener, or the middle act. Unless you have a really unique take on it, you may not be able to do that material. Plus, it's been done on Letterman and Leno and the audience may think, "Oh, here comes another one." So, as a headliner, you must rely on your own unique material.[51]

Fritz Coleman agrees and adds:

> We are all looking at the same world. As the headliner, you have the biggest stock of material, so typically you have to make the adjustments. When I'm working in a new place with a new comic, I'll try to watch the first night. It's not so much for specific jokes, but rather for the subject matter that he or she covers.[15]

Diane Nichols also reports that she likes to see the opening act on the first night of a gig. Nichols adds:

> That way, I can see if any material conflicts. I can edit it out, or I will just reflect on it and say, "Remember when so and so was talking about X?" Or, I will drop my bit if it's too close to what they do. Some headliners make the opening act drop it, but I will usually drop it. Unless it's my closer, then,

> the opener's going to have to give it up.[4]

Maintaining your "identity" when you follow a dirty or high-energy act is another challenge confronting headliners. Paul Provenza explains:

> Sometimes, I'll be on a show with a wacky guy shoving things up his nose, and I've got to follow that. The middle act has taken the audience in a certain direction for thirty minutes, and it can be a real challenge to get the audience to follow your train of thought. You may want to accomplish something in your show, but the audience has been affected by the person before who has set a tone or aroused certain instincts. You have to maintain your identity and pick up the pieces.
>
> I just said to myself, "Well, these are the cards that fate has dealt me. Let me learn how to deal with this." You are basically saying to the audience, "This is what *I* am going to do. Stay with me on this. I'm funny, too."[37]

Fritz Coleman agrees and adds that under those circumstances:

> You go out there and think of the dignity of your act and the dignity of your craft. Ultimately, you have to ap-

> proach it with the confidence you have in your act and in your material. You take charge. You let the audience know, up front, that *you* are going to be different.[15]

Paul Provenza describes some of the remedies that the headliner has at his disposal when he follows an incompatible act. Provenza states:

> You can try to defuse things right away. If I follow someone who does song parodies, I might come up and say to the audience, "Get this right off the bat. I ain't singing sh--. You're not going to hear one note out of me." Or, if it's a really filthy comic, I have a good stock line I use. I say, "Let's have another hand for so and so. He's been working on his next *Tonight Show* spot. You'll be seeing a lot of that material on television real soon. Be sure and tune in."[37]

Holding confidence in one's "funny" and one's material is also a challenge when a headliner must follow a celebrity. For example, one night comedian Steve McGrew had to follow Brad Garrett on stage at the Ice House. The audience was very excited to see Brad who portrayed a beloved character, Robert, on *Everybody Loves Raymond* for nine years. Brad did very well in his guest spot, and the audience was highly energized. Then, Steve McGrew went up on stage to close the show, and he simply began to do *his* material. In short order, McGrew had turned the crowd around and made them his. He did this by staying calm, remaining confident in his talent and material, and by giving a very strong performance.

Diane Nichols uses several sports analogies to describe some other challenges that comics face on stage. Nichols states:

> We're like ice skaters. You can really fail big and you are all alone. There is nobody to pick you up.
>
> We're also like tennis players because we never know what side the audience is on. It can go back and forth. The audience goes, "Prove you're funny." And, they judge whether you are funny against the person before you.
>
> Finally, we're like baseball players, because no matter how good you are today, tomorrow you have another game. And, another game after that.[4]

Another challenge for headliners is dealing with the theft of their material. Diane Nichols provides the following example:

> It's hard to talk to people who are not in stand-up and hear them tell me who's "good," when that person is really the biggest thief who ever walked the face of the earth. I mean guys who are doing everybody else's act. The thieves are

> usually loners. They know right off the bat they are going to pull stuff, so they never get too close to anybody.[(4)]

Other challenges/irritations for the headliner are comics who will alienate an audience by saying, "Hey, you guys stink." As one comic describes it, "The middle comic may rip the crowd to shreds before you go on, and then you are left to pick up the pieces."[(4)]

Sometimes, club owners can be a challenge for headliners. Diane Nichols illustrates:

> Some club owners make it a tough week. Not getting paid. Getting bad checks. Changing your status to pay you less. There are owners who don't know or care about talent, just that they fill the seats. Some owners have bizarre lists of rules. One actually had "take a shower before the show" on the list! Mostly though, it's labor/management stuff. They're never going to love you like your mother did.[(4)]

Club owner Bob Fisher offers the following observation regarding the relationship between comics and club owners:

> Comics and club owners are like wildebeests and lions. Are comics taken advantage of? Yes. Are there club owners who are struggling to stay open and pay their bills? Yes. Are there multi-millionaire club owners who do not pay fair wages? Yes. And,

> are there comics who make it big and then forget that they learned their craft and paid their dues at comedy clubs? Yes. The lack of respect can work both ways.

Audiences who only want dirty material can be very challenging for comics who prefer to make audiences think. Eddie Merrill explains:

> Audiences at some clubs I had to work were unsophisticated. They were intelligent, but I had one guy say to me, "If I wanted to hear those kinds of jokes, I could turn on the TV." I asked him what kinds of jokes he wanted. It was a very gutter-level type of comedy which, unfortunately, some audiences like.[21]

The comics also mention the challenge of keeping the quality of their shows consistent over the course of the week. Jeff Garcia explains:

> By Sunday, you are worn out. You've done two or three shows the night before, and two shows the night before that. So, you want to make sure that the edge is still there for the Sunday show. I think it is important to give the audience the same energy and the same me. So, I try to "anchor" the weekend with great shows. I try to make sure that the Thursday and Sunday shows are good.[53]

Another challenge for comics can be deciding when it's appropriate to perform jokes about sensitive topics or tragic events. As one comedienne describes it:

> We comics don't want to do it, but we are addicted to making jokes. We'll shuffle to the back bar, and eventually someone will mumble something about the horrible tragedy and the writers will start writing jokes about it. It's like a tick with us. We feel embarrassed, and we know it's too soon; but, first we write the jokes, then we talk about how long is an appropriate amount of time before we can do the jokes. Our minds are constantly looking for the humor or play on words.[20]

Discrimination based on age represents another challenge for veteran comics. As one comic describes it:

> There is a lot of politics in comedy, and you do feel a backlash around age. After being a comic for almost thirty years, it is hard to hear people say, "You're not young enough for the crowds we're getting in our clubs now. We only want younger comics, or 'alternative' comics, or whomever is considered hip to laugh at, at the moment."[47]

Finally, because the headliner does the most time, he is more likely to confront the challenge of unexpected emergencies during a live performance. Steve Altman observes,

"It's always fun when the microphone goes dead or the power goes out. The main thing is to keep everybody calm. You just have to be in the moment."

Comic Steve McGrew recalls the following experiences when the power has gone out:

> During one show the power went out and they actually pointed flashlights at me. At another show in Detroit, a car had hit a power line down the street and the club's power went out. The way the club was set up, they opened the two back doors, and they shined car headlights on me during the show.(44)

Steve Altman provides the following example of a headliner managing an electrical problem at the club that was potentially very serious:

> One time I was doing my act and I heard people whispering, and I thought, "Am I losing them?" Then, I saw that they were all pointing up. I looked up at the light bank and it was on fire, right above the first row of people. And, I thought, "Well, this is all f---ed up." So, I climbed on a chair and a table and I blew the flame out. I got this huge applause, and then went back on stage and finished the show."(51)

Several comics report having an audience member who had a heart attack while they were performing.[44, 54, 55] Veteran comic John Fox recalls having a man die in the audience while he was on stage:

> I was on stage and I was killing, and this guy suddenly fell out of his chair. His wife stood up and started kicking him and saying "get up" because she thought he had fallen out of his chair laughing; but, he was actually having a heart attack. Well, there were 300 people in the room who were laughing hysterically at the couple, and I'm thinking, "I'm killing this guy!" Then, someone in the back yelled, "I think he's having a heart attack," and the whole room went silent. The man literally died right then and there.[55]

Radio personality and comedian Fraser Smith recalled yet another type of emergency that had to be handled with aplomb—and a comic touch:

> One time Tom McTigue was headlining at the Ice House in Pasadena. Everyone was laughing, and there was a woman with really big hair in the crowd. She was laughing so hard that when she leaned back, her hair caught on fire from the candle on the table in back of her. All of a sudden, about twenty glasses of water were hurled at this woman from all

> directions, literally drenching her. The smell of burning hair was really bad. There was a big cloud of smoke around her. This happened about the time when Michael Jackson's hair had caught on fire while he was at a rehearsal. So, Tom McTigue paused, thought about the situation, and said, "No Michael Jackson impressions, please!"(50)

Finally, Kathy Buckley recalls her experience with an audience member who went into convulsions one evening:

> I jumped off the stage and rolled the man on his side. After I took care of him, I got back on stage. I had to recapture the audience, so, I said, "Look, if you don't like the show, just say so. You don't have to throw a fit!" Then, I said, "I hate to have to tell you guys this, but I never learned how to do CPR!"(63)

<u>Making a Living as a Headliner</u>

Up until the headliner stage, it can still be a challenge to make a living at comedy for many comics. Tom Ryan, with two Letterman appearances, explains:

> What killed me over the years is the money situation. I struggled financially for fifteen years. Now, I am finally over that hump. I am finally starting

> to make some good money. I'm real lucky to have found the corporate circuit. I tend to appeal to the corporate crowd. They pay well, and it has kept me out of debt.[64]

In addition to working in comedy clubs, some headliners perform on cruise ships. Some write for TV sitcoms or do audience warm-up for TV shows. Other comics perform regularly in variety clubs and casinos. Some headliners work in commercials or do voiceover work in films. Still other comics do promotional work where they will go out to a sporting event and do product giveaways.

At the headliner stage, the comics work on securing additional television exposure (*The Late, Late Show*, Comedy Central, etc.). Some comics work international bookings. Many take pride in having entertained the troops in the Middle East.

Until the comic's "big break," however, he typically works the comedy club circuit. He continues to hone his craft and upgrade his business skills. In addition to performing, some comedians choose to pursue related entrepreneurial efforts such as producing and pitching pilots (Vic Dunlop), writing (Jeff Cesario), and acting (Richard Belzer). Some own and/or operate a club (Gabe Kaplan, Chris Mazzilli).

<u>"Washing Out"</u>

Some headliners re-evaluate their commitment to the craft, and some "wash out" or voluntarily choose to leave performing. As comic Steve McGrew recalls:

> I've seen a lot of people wash out over the years. They'll say, "I just don't want to do this anymore." "It's not what I thought it was going to be." "I'm not moving along as fast as I thought I should have." Or, "I just got married, and it's not worth the struggle on the road." Sometimes people will even get a big break early on, and then they just disappear.[44]

Comic Rick Sandack reports that:

> People drop out if they are not making money or getting jobs. If the word is out that you are not funny, you start to get the message. You start taking other jobs and you perform less and less. You just sort of fade out.[6]

Billy Gardell describes two other reasons that a comic might drop out:

> There are a couple of traps on the road. Drugs and alcohol for one. Another is having a crazy night, and someone ends up pregnant. You have to learn how to control yourself. You have to learn how to skate through all that stuff, or you may wash out.[65]

Finally one comedienne describes the decision to leave stand-up comedy after eight years of performing this way:

> You know, I know, and the other comics know that I'm good. But, I've

been told, over and over, that I look one way and sound another. I don't fit. They don't know what to do with me. I'm not what people are commercially interested in right now. I'm somebody that people really laugh at, but I don't have the talent coordinators and development people coming around to make me the next star.

At first, there was disillusionment and then a sense of reconciliation. It was in that order, like the stages of death, actually: Denial, Anger, Depression, and then, finally, Acceptance.

I've gone as far as I can go for right now. I don't get to go on to the next level. My husband always wanted to move, but my career always kept us from going. So, I've decided to move.

I also realized that it's never been okay to just be me. I've always had to be me in a big way in order to validate my existence. Most people say, "How do you perform on stage?" But, the hardest thing for me is to just be me.

I know that I could go to the Bay area and get on stage. And, I could get a lot of attention and make a lot of money if I choose. But, that would be

> easy. For me, anonymity will be the challenge.[20]

Superstardom: A Desired Outcome of Headlining

Among comics, a chosen few move onto superstardom. Some comics pursue their big break through comedy competitions such as *Star Search* and *Last Comic Standing*. These avenues provide prize money and national exposure previously available only through spots on *Letterman* and *Leno*. Even if one does not win, exposure on such competitions results in more work, better bookings, and higher salaries. These programs also secure "name brand" recognition for the comic (e.g., Alonzo Bodden, Ant). Many of these comics then tour individually and with others from the show.

Other comics pursue career advancement through local and national comedy competitions such as the Montreal Comedy Festival, the Johnny Walker Comedy Competition, and the San Francisco Comedy Competition. For example, Rocky LaPorte's career got a major boost after winning the Johnny Walker national contest, and Alonzo Bodden's headlining career was launched after he won the New Faces competition at the Montreal Comedy Festival. Bodden recalls:

> I went in as a "new face," and came out a headliner with TV money. But, the best part was the respect and congratulations from people like Dom Irrera and Barry Katz who knew me when I was a doorman at the Laugh Factory. When Dom Irrera says you're funny, you're funny![55]

Still other comics secure jobs as radio personalities (e.g., Steve McGrew in Colorado; Willie Barcena and Larry Omaha in Sacramento). Such comics often come to Los Angeles to perform on Fridays and Saturdays. In this way, they are able to audition, work out new material in front of live audiences, and maintain industry ties in addition to having a another job.

Some comics are tapped to host television shows (Bob Saget, Joe Rogan, Louie Anderson). Other comics work as regulars in sitcoms (e.g., Blake Edwards in *Home Improvement* and Tim O'Rourke on *The Drew Carey Show*). Still other performers headline or perform regularly in Las Vegas (e.g., Rita Rudner, Diane Ford).

A few comics secure very successful cable TV deals (Dave Chappelle, Gary Shandling), and a handful achieve the dream of starring in their own network television sit-com (e.g., Jerry Seinfeld, George Lopez, Ray Romano, Drew Carey, Tim Allen, Kevin James, and Damon Wayans). Some comedians move on to a career in movies (e.g., Jim Carrey and Robin Williams).

This level of success also opens the door for the comic to do HBO specials and headline at the largest venues across the country. Stand-up comedians such as Larry the Cable Guy, Jeff Foxworthy, George Lopez, and Dave Chappelle generate big business from performing in large venues. Such concerts have also spawned comedy DVDs (*The Blue Collar Comedy Tour*), and CDs that have debuted high on the Billboard chart (e.g., Dane Cook).

Of course, such successes have followed roughly twenty years of "paying one's dues." Jerry Seinfeld, George Lopez, and Ray Romano et al. each worked in clubs all over the country, week after week, year after year. They painstakingly learned the craft, committed to the art, learned to write comedy, built a following, built a "brand" name, and learned to navigate the business aspects of comedy over that period.

Some Words of Wisdom for Working Comics

For those club comics who have not yet become "superstars," comedian Kathy Buckley offers the following advice:

> Don't compare yourself with another comic. Continue to work on your own act. If somebody is doing better than you are, take a look at what they are doing right. Learn from that. Don't begrudge somebody else's success or be angry.
>
> Listen to your audience. Listen to your critics. Take the feedback for what it's worth. Don't beat yourself up; and, see what you can get out of constructive criticism that can help you to improve.[63]

Tom Ryan provides the following tips for headliners:

> Enjoy the craft. Be proud of your work. Then, let the chips fall where they may. Instead of bitterness and jealousy, think of others' success this way: "I can do that well in my career, too!"[64]

Billy Gardell has the following recommendations for working comics:

> Waste all your money and all your time the first five years. Then, start planning for retirement as though you are never going to become a superstar. Invest, save your money, or look for lateral ways to make money in this profession such as writing, being a radio personality, or being a talk show host. Don't worry about becoming a "superstar." If it happens great; but, first worry about making a living.[65]

Finally, Rudy Moreno offers these words of wisdom to comics of all stages:

> It all depends on what your intention is as a comic. If your intention is to become a star, the reality is that the chances of that are very slim. A lot of this is luck.
>
> As long as you understand that, and you are willing to take that risk, then this job is for you. But, if you are thinking, "In five years I'm going to have my own TV show," think again. They don't hand them out like that.
>
> If you are in it for the art, for the fun, or even for the "chicks," then you'll be okay. If you can learn to handle hecklers, club owners, and personality

> clashes with other comics, and also practice your craft, you can very well headline. If you are good enough to be a headliner at a club and get TV exposure, that is, for the majority of comics, success.[43]

Barbara's Closing Thoughts

Comedians are an imaginative, talented, extremely fun-loving, and often hard-living group of men and women whose identity is closely bound to a need for an intense emotional connection with others on a large scale. Their need for approval, a feeling of power, and a connection with others outweighs even their deepest fear–and their experience–of rejection by audiences. In most cases, the comedy they share with us is also infused with a genuine, life-long love for entertaining others.

Comics can be profane and vulgar. They can be brilliant social observers, and they can be incisive social critics. Some comics prefer shock value and like to push the boundaries of convention with their material; others work more quietly, subtly, and with a great deal of charm and poignancy. Some comics demonstrate a variety of talents (e.g., impressions, singing, juggling). There are some genuinely nice guys and gals in the business, and there are some comics who have serious problems with alcohol and drugs. There are some very smart businessmen, and there are those for whom dysfunction reins. As a group, comics live—and work—close to their impulses. This often serves them well on stage; sometimes, not so well off stage.

Comics can be very competitive, but they are also there for one another in countless ways. Their bond is humor—and the many difficult challenges they face in doing the work they love. Ironically, their job comes at a very high cost to many of them in terms of personal unhappiness, difficulty finding work, and difficulty maintaining stable relationships.

Stand-up is like a calling or vocation. There is almost a compulsion to perform on stage for comedians: some feel "most fulfilled" or "most alive" when they are performing. Stand-up is a job that is, at once, extremely gratifying and overwhelmingly depressing. It is deceptively difficult and emotionally demanding. As many comedians describe it, "It's a tough life." Comic Charlie Hill speaks for many comedians when he asserts, "Comedy is the hardest to do, and it is the least respected." Indeed, the intricacies of the craft are invisible if they are done well, and the art form is not fully appreciated for precisely that reason.

Over the course of their training, stand-up comics learn *exceptional* writing and editing skills. They develop *keen insights* into audiences. They learn *remarkable* audience interaction skills, and they become *masters* of crowd management. They also perfect performing techniques that make stand-up only *look* easy.

Compared to a formal, rigorous, medical school curriculum, the craft of stand-up is largely learned informally, through individual effort, and by trial and error. The "instruction" that does occur takes often place on stage in front of audiences and in the green room, where the ins and outs of the craft are discussed, debated, and passed down from one comic to another.

Simply put, comics are a group among us who have taken their natural ability for making others laugh and honed it to *an art*. The more the comics shared about their work, the more committed I became to documenting their craft. I hope the reader has come away with a better understanding of stand-up comedy as a performance art, what it takes to be a comedian, and just how fragile a performance can be.

In closing, remember that the comedian's standing invitation to audiences is to *laugh*. To that I would only add: *Enjoy the performance,* and don't "*trip the ballerina!*"

CHAPTER 6

GIGS FROM HELL

Who Booked This Gig?

The funniest thing that happened to me on stage was when I first started out. Some other comics and I did a gig at a retirement home. We got there, and these were not people in their 60s; these were people in their late 80s. I first realized I was in trouble when I saw a record album lying around titled, *The Top Hits from the 1920s.* There were four comics who went up, and we all just bombed. People were falling asleep. Their oxygen masks were half falling off. Some of the residents thought we were magicians. Plus, these people had grown up in a different time in the evolution of racism. I'm Vietnamese, and we had two Latino comics and a Chinese comic on the line up. They really didn't "get" our ethnic humor, and they all just looked confused. They were staring at us as if we were selling insurance or something. But, as I was performing, out of the corner of my eye I could see the comics behind the curtain laughing so hard they were rolling on the floor. We might as well have been playing to an empty room. So, we just started performing for each other.

- Dat Phan

What Other Performing Artist Would Tolerate This?

I performed in San Francisco at a club one time. I thought it was going to be a great gig and a hip crowd. There were about thirty people, but I sucked and they sucked, and I just died on stage. I figured the next crowd would be different, so I asked the manager when they were going to turn the room over. He said, "No, it's the same crowd." I said, "but I have another forty-five minutes to do!" He said, "Do it again. They don't care.'"

- Charlie Hill

The Kind of Show You Never Forget

One night I performed at a University for 2,000 college students during Greek Week. It was the biggest crowd I had ever performed for. About fifteen minutes into my act, one guy way in the back started to boo. And then, the heckling slowly started to spread. I could feel the panic rise. I filled my time, but I just wasn't getting any laughs. By the end of my set, the students were starting to sing, "Na, Na, Na, Na, Hey, Hey, Hey, Goodbye."

- Tom Ryan

Umm, Why Bother Booking a Comedian?

I did a company Christmas party in 2007. They wanted a comedian, but nothing was set up for a comedy show. There was no stage. There was a huge open dance floor. They had a DJ. They had all of these raunchy games set up. After dinner, the DJ walks over to me and says, "Are you ready?" And I said "Now?" People had gotten up from their tables. They were talking among themselves. So, then the DJ announces me. There was a line for the open bar that was so long the last person in line was blocking me from half of the room. People were walking back and forth. The servers were bringing out dessert and passing right in front of me. People were heckling, and I couldn't respond to them as I would in a club. And, I had to do forty-five minutes. I was paid a lot of money to show up, but it was a nightmare.

- James P. Connolly

GIGS FROM HELL - CONT'D

What Could She Have Been Thinking?

About three years ago, I was playing a one-nighter at a college in Kentucky. One girl in the front row kept heckling everybody. She heckled the radio DJ. She heckled the MC. She heckled the middle act so bad that he almost cried. He literally said to her, "Lady, will you let me do my show? You're embarrassing me in front of all these people."

I went up on stage and said, "I won't deal with your sh—" She said, "What? Yes, you will." She continued to bad-mouth me, and I finally made a really rude comment. She had one of those big banana hair clips and I said, "What is that clip for? To hold in the little bit of brains you have so they don't fall out?" The guy with her said, "You don't talk to a lady like that." I said, "I wouldn't talk to a lady like that, but she is not a lady." So, then he came at the stage, and I kicked him in the chest and knocked him back. His two buddies stood up and came toward the stage. The bouncers were there by then, and I picked up the mic and said, "Thanks to this woman, your show is over." I dropped the mic and walked off.

- Anonymous

Did Somebody Say "Food Fight!"?

One time I did a gig in the South for a liquor distributor. They had a contest where whoever came up and told the funniest joke was going to win money. However, everybody was drunk. Right when I went on stage, some lady yelled an obscenity; I didn't even get to say, "Hi." Immediately, I thought, "Oh, this is going to be bad." So, this lady went up on stage to tell her joke, and people were starting to boo her and they were starting to throw napkins. I was losing control, and I said, "Give me the mic!" and she said "No!"

You could feel the tension rising in the room and then all hell broke loose. It literally turned into a college food fight. I was trying to get the microphone away from this lady. We fell on the floor, and we were wrestling around for the microphone. People were throwing things.

But, the funniest part of it was that the president of the company came up to me and said, "That was great!" He even gave me a $600 cash bonus! I thought, "I didn't even do anything! I assaulted one of your employees! I had to take down one of your people to get the mic!"

- Anonymous

A Comedy Show—Straight from the Coal Mines?

One time I booked a Halloween gig in West Virginia. On a map, it looked to be about three hours away from where I lived; however, with all the winding roads, it took us about six hours to get to the gig. The club turned out to be an old bowling alley—with the ball returns pulled up. The PA system consisted of a small podium mic and a pin mic that you clipped on your collar. Around 7:00 p.m., the girls arrived in their Halloween costumes. Later, their dates arrived—faces blackened, covered in coal dust, straight from the mines. We ended up working in Lane 14. The girls just wanted to dance and the guys were extremely tired, and it just seemed like total silence during our entire performance.

- Tim O'Rourke

CHAPTER 6

GIGS FROM HELL - CONT'D

Is "One Person" Considered an Audience?

One time, early in my career, I went on stage and there was literally one man in the audience. I stood there thinking, "Why are you here? Why are you alone? Why would you stay? Why am I on stage right now? If you left, I wouldn't have to come up here and try to have a conversation with you holding a microphone." Later, one of the older comics was trying to be encouraging and said, "As you go along, you'll find that sometimes small crowds are more fun than big crowds." And, I thought, "That's not a crowd; that's a dude!"

- John Caparulo

Another Reason You May Not Want to Sit in the Front Row at a Comedy Show

I had a 102-degree fever one time in Fort Lauderdale, Florida. I couldn't get my nose to stop running. I took some cold medicines and nothing was working. Then, while I was on stage, I sneezed—and out shot a wad of nasal drip all over the front row. I think the audience laughed for about ten minutes. In fact, it may be the best laugh I've ever gotten. And, I just couldn't recover; I had to say goodnight after that. Once you've sneezed on an audience, that's pretty much it. Nothing I could do was going to top that.

- Anonymous

"Collateral Damage" from 9/11

My gig from hell took place on 9/11. I was scheduled to do two shows on a cruise ship. First of all, I was depressed: I didn't know if my sister was safe because no calls could go through in New York that day. Second, the passengers on the ship were mostly New Yorkers returning from the Caribbean. All day, they had been watching the same edited footage of Tower 1 then Tower 2 collapsing. Everyone was worried about his or her family and friends. Some people were angry. To make matters worse, right before my comedy show they decided to observe two minutes of silence. Then, the announcer said, "And now...here's your comic." It was the worst introduction and the worst combination of events I've ever faced. I just went up and talked about what was going on, and tried to make the best of a very difficult situation.

- Chris Clobber

Just Remember: Six Strangers Don't Determine How Talented You Are

The most difficult gig I had was the first time I hosted a show. I was 22. I had been doing "open mics" for a couple of years, and I was asked to host a weekend show at a small club in Baltimore. It was the first show Friday night. There were six people in the audience. They were all seated at one table. I started doing my jokes and they hated me. They didn't laugh at a single thing I said. I could literally hear the crunching of the nachos. This was my first time hosting and I had so hoped it was a step forward. But when it went so badly, I literally started to think, "Maybe I shouldn't be doing comedy." The second show there were 30 or 40 people. I did okay. It wasn't great, but it gave me some confidence to continue. That first show sure was devastating though.

- K.T. Tatara

PRESSURES, PRESSURES, PRESSURES

- Not working enough/hustling for jobs/struggling to make a living.

- Knowing that you are good, better than some, and you are still having difficulty getting on at certain clubs.

- The great sets "juice" the ego; the bad sets depress, and you must find a balance.

- Trying to be perfect, during a brief time, at something that is very difficult—knowing that all of your hard work can go down the drain with the slip of a performance. "Just when you think you've got an audience, they veer to the right!"

- Being alone on a stage with only your brains, your wit, and your courage—in front of an audience that can be a fickle monster. You never know.

- Having to find the way to the heart of each audience, and find a way to overcome the barriers that divide the comic's mind from the audience's.

- Having to please owners, bookers, and talent executives who have their own agendas and objectives over which you have no control.

- Having to put on a "game face" for an audience and pretend to be happy and self-confident, even if one is unhappy.

- Constantly having to be on the alert for the comic possibilities in everything, storing them for later use.

- Managing emotional reactions to material that is very personal and painful to re-live, while you are on stage trying to be funny.

- Being in a business in which so much is on the line with each deal—big money, clout, credibility, and leverage for subsequent deals.

- Drastic shifts in social relations, i.e., one day you are nothing to someone, the next day they want to be your best friend. One day you are on top and the next day you are a "has been."

- Being in a business that treats the performer like property. Studios set demanding schedules and pressure the performer to perform in or produce shows that conflict with the performer's standards or beliefs (art vs. corporate interests). There is also a tendency to move on to the next "hot property" when a performer "cools," a deal falls through, or somebody "bigger" enters the scene.

- As a headliner, you have to work hard so you continue to be a draw and put people's butts in seats. You must do everything in your power to reach an audience through various media outlets (radio, television, newspapers, etc.)[101]

- You must learn how to respond to any situation, e.g., with radio personalities who just like to hear themselves talk or just want to move on to the next record, and you learn how to fit into a talk show with five other people.[101]

- You always have to be ready for the next audition and for the next showcase. You have to juggle performances, meetings, theatrical agents commercial agents, college agents, your manager, and your family.[84]

List of Comics Interviewed

1. Bill Kalmenson
2. Bruce Mahler
3. Jim Shubert
4. Diane Nichols
5. Ralph Valdez
6. Rick Sandack
7. Jason Stuart
8. Karen Haber
9. Steve Carey
10. Frank Carrasquillo
11. Karen Wyeth
12. Tim Jones
13. John Caponera
14. Jeff Altman
15. Fritz Coleman
16. Felice Miller
17. Argus Hamilton
18. Steven Allen Green
19. Lou Adams, Ph.D.
20. Karen Babbitt
21. Eddie Merrill
22. Sally Edwards, correspondence
23. Jeffrey Peterson
24. Paul Dillery
25. Ron Richards
26. Robin Cee
27. John Roarke
28. John Wing
29. Rick Overton
30. Bruce Mikelson
31. Peter Johnson
32. Jeff Cesario
33. Charlie Hill

34. Yakov Smirnov
35. Kathy Ladman
36. Gary Muledeer
37. Paul Provenza
38. Valerie Pappas
39. Jimmy Burns
40. Jimmy Brogan
41. Ant
42. Rocky LaPorte
43. Rudy Moreno
44. Steve McGrew
45. Jarrod Cardwell
46. Nick Gaza
47. Vic Dunlop
48. Darren Carter
49. Michael Jr.
50. Frazer Smith
51. Steve Altman
52. Joey Gaynor
53. Jeff Garcia
54. Kevin Jordan
55. Alonzo Bodden
56. John Fox
57. Charlie Laborte
58. Robin Cee
59. Darryl Sivad
60. Jason Stuart
61. Dan Smith
62. Larry Omaha
63. Kathy Buckley
64. Tom Ryan
65. Billy Gardell
66. Tammy Pescatelli
67. Daniel Nainan
68. Margaret Smith
69. Joey Medina

70. Don Friesen

71. John Caparulo

72. James P. Connolly

73. Charles Sanchez

74. Dat Phan

75. Kareem

76. Juan Canopii

77. Fred Burns

78. Joan Fagan

79. Andres Fernandez

80. Willis Turner

81. Mike Estime

82. Maryellen Hooper

83. Johnnie Cardinale

84. Kivi Rogers

85. Gilbert Esquivel

86. Andre Chemene

87. Spanky (Steven Kent McFarland)

88. Alex Reymundo

89. Ian Bagg

90. Ari Shafir

91. Lou Santini

92. Frank Nicotero

93. Michael Pace

94. Eric Blake

95. Armando Cosio

96. Steve Bluestein

97. Tim O'Rourke

98. Christine Sparta

99. K.T. Tatara

100. Chris Clobber

101. Craig Shoemaker

BIBLIOGRAPHY

Allen, Steve. *Funny People*
New York: Stein and Day, 1981

Allen, Steve. *More Funny People*
New York: Stein and Day, 1982

Berger, Phil. *The Last Laugh: The World of the Stand-Up Comic.*
New York: William Morrow and Company, Inc., 1975

Berle, Milton. *Milton Berle: An Autobiography*
New York: Delacorte Press, 1974

Borns, Betsy. *Comic Lives: Inside the World of American Stand-Up Comedy*
New York: Simon and Shuster, 1987

Brenner, David. *Soft Pretzels with Mustard*
New York: Arbor House, 1983

Cavett, Richard A and Christopher Porterfield. *Dick Cavett*
New York: Harcourt, Brace, Johanovich, 1974

Croy, Homer. *Our Will Rogers*
New York: Duell, Sloan, and Pearce, 1953

Ephron, Nora. *And Now, Here's Johnny*
New York: Avon Books, 1968

Fine, Irving. *Jack Benny*
New York: GP Putnam, 1976

Franklin, Joe. *Joe Franklin's Encyclopedia of Comedians*
Secaucus, New Jersey: Citadel Press, 1979

Goldman, Albert. *Ladies and Gentlemen, Lenny Bruce*
New York: Random House, 1974

Maltin, Leonard. *The Great Movie Comedians*
Crown Publishers. 1978

Sahl, Mort. *Heartland*
New York: Harcourt, Brace, Johanovich, 1976

Smith, Ron. *Cosby*
New York: St. Martin's Press, 1986

Woodward, Bob. *The Short Life and Fast Times of John Belushi*
New York: Simon and Schuster, 1984

Made in the USA